Children, Teachers and Learning Series

General Editor: Cedric Cullingford

Teaching Music in the Primary School

Second Edition

Titles in the *Children, Teachers and Learning* series:

Teaching Music in the Primary School

Second Edition

Edited by Joanna Glover and
Stephen Ward

 continuum
LONDON • NEW YORK

This book is dedicated to Dorothy
and
to Zoë and Fran

Continuum

The Tower Building	15 East 26th Street
11 York Road	New York
London SE1 7NX	NY 10010

© The editors and contributors 1993, 1998

First edition published 1993. Reprinted 1996. Second edition 1998.
Second edition reprinted 2004

British Library Cataloguing-in-Publication Data
A catalogue record for this book is available from the British Library

ISBN 0-304-70282-X (hardback)
       0-826-47818-2 (paperback)

Typeset by Fakenham Photosetting Limited, Fakenham, Norfolk.
Printed and bound in Great Britain by
Antony Rowe Ltd, Chippenham, Wiltshire

Contents

About this book

The first edition of this book was written in 1991 when the National Curriculum for music was emerging. Those were exciting times when, for the first time, all children would have the entitlement to an education which would include performing, composing, listening to music; primary music was destined to grow from simply *singing in the hall*. In the years that have elapsed since then, great strides have been made and many of the recommendations which we made in our first edition are now happening in schools: for example, children's musical composition is becoming a part of the normal school day and music is being taught effectively by class teachers who are supported by a music co-ordinator.

This book looks at the nature of children's learning in music in the context of current thinking in primary education. It is intended to help all primary teachers to develop children's music in their classrooms and those with a co-ordinating role who support them.

Chapter 1 discusses the way we think about music itself and the changes needed if children's music is to be placed at the centre of the music curriculum. Chapter 2 looks at music teaching in the context of primary practice and tells the story of the development of the National Curriculum for primary music with all its twists and turns and political debates.

The processes underlying the activities of performing, composing, listening and appraising on which the music curriculum is built are discussed in Chapter 3, and ways of assessing children's music in the National Curriculum are examined in Chapter 4.

Chapters 5 and 6 are written by primary teachers and give a practical perspective on how music can be managed in the classroom at Key Stage 1 and Key Stage 2. These chapters would be a good introduction to any class teachers who are working in music with children for the first time.

Children's composition is the newest area of growth in primary school music. Chapter 7 looks at the nature of children's composition and how teachers can develop it in the classroom.

Music should now be seen as part of the whole primary curriculum. The fact that it is now taught by class teachers means that it can become an integral part, rather than a stand-alone subject taught by specialists. Chapter 8 examines the links between music and other areas in the curriculum, giving practical examples and activities to help planning. In doing this we discuss the nature of music as a subject in itself.

The final chapter is written for those with the role of subject leader or music co-ordinator in the primary school and discusses the skills required of anyone teaching music. It draws on the authors' experience in supporting teachers who are training as co-ordinators. A range of strategies for leadership and co-ordination is offered.

Acknowledgements

We are grateful to all the students and teachers who have helped to shape our thinking about music. Particular thanks are due to all the tutors, teachers and advisers involved with the South West Regional Primary Music Consultancy Course and the DFEE Courses for Curriculum Co-ordinators run at Bath Spa University College.

In addition we wish to thank:

> Marie Coombes and the staff of Eastville Junior School, Bristol

> The staff of May Park Primary School, Bristol, Bannerman Road Primary School, Bristol, and St Saviour's Infants School, Bath

> Gillian Atkinson, Grove Junior School, Nailsea, Bristol

and all the children for their music.

The extract from 'The Dry Salvages', in *The Four Quartets* by T.S. Eliot, is reproduced by permission of Faber and Faber Ltd.

About the contributors

Lesley Flash trained as a Montessori teacher and worked in experimental schools in the UK and USA before joining the UK state-maintained system. She has worked as a reception class teacher at St Saviour's Infants School, Bath, and with initial and inservice training students on professional studies music courses at Bath Spa University College.

Joanna Glover lectures in music and music education at Bath Spa University College where she runs initial and inservice courses and consultancy work in music education. Her particular interests are in children's composition and the philosophy of music. She edits, with Susan Young, the journal *Primary Music Today*. Also with Susan Young she is the co-author of two books: *Music in the Early Years* and *Primary Music: Later Years*, both published by Falmer Press.

Stephen Ward is Head of Primary Education at Bath Spa University College. His particular interests are in children's language and literacy, developments in primary education, and partnership with teachers and schools in initial teacher education. He has edited, with David Coulby, *The Primary Core National Curriculum*, published by Cassell.

Susan Young currently lectures in music education at the Roehampton Institute. She was formerly a class teacher at Wrington CE Primary School, Avon, and at the Wells Cathedral School. With Joanna Glover she is co-editor of *Primary Music Today* and co-author of *Music in the Early Years* and *Primary Music: Later Years*, both published by Falmer Press.

CHAPTER 1
Understanding Music
Joanna Glover and Stephen Ward

Introduction

There is nothing exceptional about being musical. Everyone is. For various reasons some people are exceptionally musical, just as some are exceptionally mathematical or athletic. Some people don't *feel* musical at all, or would hesitate in describing themselves as such, perhaps because they have no expertise on an instrument or because they have been told they can't sing. Yet being musical is quite simply one aspect of being human. This book is concerned with music as a part of the main curriculum for all children throughout the primary school. Music learning is seen as essentially classroom and class-teacher based within the context of a whole-school musical life.

The commercial music world offers, at the touch of a switch, a dazzling array of polished performances and recordings by professional composers, song-writers and musicians. Amateur music, in orchestras, bands and choirs, also demands a high level of performance. It is understandable, then, that primary teachers sometimes find it hard to see how anything which approaches this can be managed in the primary classroom situation. Noise, limited time and resources, perhaps their own and the children's lack of vocal and instrumental skills, all seem to conspire against any really musical outcome in the classroom. So music has tended to be seen as a specialized, even an extra-curricular, activity, led by the school's music specialist.

Yet music plays a role in almost everyone's daily life and it is this widespread engagement with music in one or other of its forms that should take its place in the picture alongside the more formal aspects of musical composition and performance. The curriculum must allow for the breadth of the role that music plays within 'ordinary' life for everyone.

The music in everyone

Music is not a language. It does, however, share some fundamental similarities with language and useful parallels can be drawn. Almost everyone is an ordinary language user and language plays both a functional and an

1

expressive part in daily life. There are language-based art forms, specialized uses of language in poetry, story, song, drama and novel, ranging from oral vernacular traditions to high art forms. Music has a similar range, from humming in the kitchen to the high art form of grand opera.

All music has its roots in the activities of ordinary daily human living. The structures of music of any level of complexity derive from these patterns: of communication by voice and gesture; of physical action in movement, work, dance or play; of interaction with each other one-to-one or as part of a group; of observing and imposing order on the world we live in – all patterns which make up our way of life. It is these relationships that underlie the universal ability to hear, make sense of and respond to musical structures whether or not we have been trained to do so. The music we hear connects with what we already know.

Continuous with these patterns are the simple forms of 'music-using' behaviour which play a functional and an expressive part in daily life for most people. These might be humming, singing known or made-up tunes or fragments, story-singing, rhythmic or repetitive work actions, finger drumming, jumping up and down, choosing music to work, dance or drive to, for listening and for relaxation, and taking part in music with others as part of worship, ceremony, and social gatherings of all kinds. In at least some of these basic ways we are all music-makers, though Western culture allows some people to become more rusty than others in exercising this capacity. We are all able to listen and respond to the music of others.

Much of this behaviour is fragmentary, passing or incidental to other activity. Yet it is closely woven into what might be called the drama of our lives, the dynamics of action and emotion, of thought and expression, and it is these contexts that give music its 'meaningfulness'. At the more organized level of the musical piece – the song, the symphony, the music drama – each musical style or genre has conventions and behaviours associated with it, as defined by social practice. Each genre has its own skills of composition, improvisation or performance and its own practices and background knowledge against which a listener understands and makes judgements about what is heard.

All of this forms a spectrum of musical activity like the spectrum of language-use mentioned above. Recognizing the breadth of this range and its continuity is important in the context of music education for two reasons. The first is that too often music teaching has assumed that music belongs to 'musicians', that only some are musical and certainly that children have to be introduced to music in school as if they were beginners without any musical experience. Such attitudes are reinforced where music is allowed to be the provenance solely of a specialist teacher and confined to a rehearsal-style lesson once a week. To maintain such an outlook entails either an extremely narrow conception of what counts as music or a deafness to a whole aspect of human behaviour. Blacking (1976, pp. 8–9) points out the paradox of treating the whole nation as musical 'consumers' whilst denying the musicality of all but a few:

> 'My' society claims that only a limited number of people are musical, and yet it behaves as if all people possessed the basic capacity without which no musical tradition can exist – the capacity to listen and distinguish patterns of sound. . . .
>
> The very existence of a professional performer, as well as his necessary financial support, depends on listeners who in one important respect must be no less musically proficient than he is. They must be able to distinguish and interrelate different patterns of sound.

In fact, all children come to school with considerable musical experience and most with their capacity for spontaneous music-making intact. All children are able to make music and respond to music. Indeed we would have to re-examine the whole idea of an entitlement music curriculum for all children if this was not the case. And all teachers, by virtue simply of being competent adults, have the musical capacity to provide a basis for a music curriculum for their own class, though they may lack the training in music education to feel confident about where to start.

The second reason why it is important to take the widest possible view of the spectrum of musical activity relates to the fundamental question of what it is to understand music. The language analogy is again useful. Understanding language involves being able to use it in a variety of contexts and for a variety of purposes. Understanding music involves being able to use it, as makers, as listeners, workers, dancers and worshippers both in ordinary, momentary ways and in more formed and formal ways, alone and with other people and for a variety of purposes. Children come to an understanding of the intrinsic qualities of music, and of the kind of thing it can do, only through encountering it right across the spectrum and being involved in it as 'users' where it belongs in a myriad of different human contexts. And it must be clear from the beginning that in the case of both language and music at a basic level these are competencies, developed in the ordinary course of things by anyone who has had the opportunity. They form the foundation on which is built all subsequent engagement in either the literary or the musical arts, as makers or as appraisers. As Wittgenstein (1967, para. 173) has it: 'Only in the stream of thought and life do words have meaning.'

So music can only make sense in the stream of action and experiences. Therefore school must be a musical microcosm, giving music its real-life contexts within which to locate the teaching of its skills and knowledge and establish continuity with the outside world at every layer from that of professional performer to that of the everyday. The teacher must have musical self esteem and let musical responses show. The teacher must develop his/her musical self.

Children's music

The great majority of children come to school as competent language users and music users. Over the last twenty years language and literacy learning in the primary classroom have taken a developmental approach in which the child's own language-use is the starting-point. Britton (1971) and Wells (1986), for example, have shown how speaking and listening are developed by drawing on the language the children already have, encouraging them to talk in a variety of contexts at their own level. The National Writing Project (Nelson, 1990) has shown how children's emergent writing leads on to composing, drafting, editing and presenting their own writing. Learning in music should start with the children's innate capacities and the experiences they bring to the classroom, building further skills and understanding from there. It follows from this that teachers need to become accustomed to *observing* children's musical behaviour as individuals and to think in terms of providing experiences which *match* a particular child's abilities and needs. This involves no more than applying to work in music those skills in observation and assessment that are used in other curriculum areas. This may be as yet unfamiliar to some teachers but with a little practice and experience of the children's work it is not hard. Chapter 7 gives detailed help with listening to and assessing children's music.

A useful beginning is to listen to the music that young children make quite regardless of whether they have been asked or taught to do so. This can be a most salutary exercise, for it shows straight away that no child of school age is ever 'starting from the beginning' in language or music. To make such a study it is necessary to take some time to observe children in a number of different environments and situations, looking first perhaps for those occasions on which spontaneous *music-making behaviour* takes place, as it does from babyhood on.

For example, when *watching and listening to* a very young child, any of the following or similar behaviour might be observed:

occasion	*musical behaviour*
in the bath	pitched babble, sometimes song
strapped into car seat	singing and banging together
playing with Lego	story singing
stamping in puddle	voice and feet rhythm

Sound-making is being enjoyed alongside other activity and is becoming organized in rhythmic and tuneful ways. (The musical elements to which these behaviours might be related are indicated in round brackets below and are explained in more detail in Chapter 5.) Listening carefully it is possible to hear:

- a wide range of sorts of voice use, voice qualities or other sorts of sounds being enjoyed for their own sake (*timbre*);
- a wide range of pitch use: ups and downs, slides and jumps, two notes alternating in sing-song (e.g. police siren) effects, one note held steady (*pitch, melody*);
- a wide range of rhythm use: rhythmic chanting, playing with speech rhythms, steady beating with body or beaters, patterned beating of shorts and longs, irregular beating (*rhythm*);
- a wide range of structures: unbroken streams of music, repetitions, doing again the same but different, verse and chorus structures (*form*).

It is this constantly evolving *music-making behaviour,* which, unless strongly discouraged, persists as a natural part of most children's play and other activity. The teacher can build on this and on the ready responsiveness children bring to music they hear from other people. Some of this behaviour may be small snatches only, fragments of tune or rhythm quickly discarded or changed to something else. Some of it may be more extended and, certainly with school-aged children, may result in improvised or composed music arrived at 'on the wing' using voices or instruments, perhaps makeshift instruments.

> Mark (aged 7) carefully arranged a complete collection of saucepan lids and other metal objects on the path in the yard. He played there with a friend for most of the afternoon, making patterns of rhythm, pitch and timbre.

Teachers have become skilled in responding to children's written work and their visual art-making. As adults, accustomed to listening mainly to music made by adults, the teacher may have to go through a process of adjustment in order to hear what's going on in children's own music, at the extreme perhaps even in order to hear it *as* music. Children are engaged in the long-term processes of growing up: processes of maturation, of acculturation and of acquiring competencies. And each of these aspects has *musical* implications which teachers need to understand since they relate to the ways in which children's music *sounds* different from adults' music.

When young children themselves start off a circle singing-game the speed they choose may be very different from that set by an adult. The speed is different because it relates to the length and speed of their steps. Music can only be understood by first recognizing the intimacy of its relationship with the sensations of living in a human body and then by recognizing it to be a very simple form of assertion, ordering and control within the immediate environment, of making sound marks on the world. Children's physical frames and movements are not the same as adults' and their music differs accordingly.

Inevitably children's music also reflects the social and cultural influences of their childhood at a particular time and place, which in itself is a powerful sub-culture, and also the stage they have reached in respect of their gradual initiation into adult social and cultural systems. Children's music is connected to adult music in these respects, but it is not the same.

It must also be recognized that, as with their work in any other sphere, children's music is shaped by the perceptions and competencies of their age and experience. Skill levels in listening, thinking, physical co-ordination and social interaction will all have a direct bearing on how their music is formed and, just as in other curriculum areas, teachers need to take account of these in coming to understand an individual's work. A corollary of this is that the music children make tells the listener a great deal about their stage of development in many respects.

The following factors may have effects on children's music:

maturation: size/weight, short legs, high voices, small lungs, fast heartbeats, baby teeth, developing muscle power, cognitive development;
acculturation: the long process of becoming initiated into adult musical styles and practices, into language/speech patterns, into forms of social interaction and organisation;
acquiring competencies: developing physical control and co-ordination, perceptual skills, intellectual understanding, the ability to co-operate with others.

Finally, music is deeply rooted in the inner sense of being: it has creative and spiritual dimensions, it is sometimes expressive, sometimes play and sometimes dance made audible. Therefore, it is to be expected that, as with any creative work children engage in, their musical art has an aesthetic value of its own. When children are involved in music-making in the classroom it must be expected to sound like *their* music, just as children's art work is expected to look like their art. In 1948 Marion Richardson wrote about the paintings of the children she taught:

How different it all was from the orthodox technique which these children had learned in imitation of adult conventional art. They were now developing an art of their own, vital enough to discover its own means of expression. (p. 17)

It is in accepting that children's music *connects with* adult music-making but is not the same that teachers can capitalize on what children bring to the classroom situation. Joan Tough (1979) pointed out that teachers needed to listen to children's spoken language; listening to their spontaneous music-making, in the classroom, playground or elsewhere, pays similar dividends. Listening and observation, rather than performance, are the central skills of teaching music and any teacher can acquire them. Indeed, in order to offer activities and learning experiences which match the children's needs it will be essential to do some such listening as part of a diagnostic process. If the children appear not to be musically active, and sometimes they have been deterred at an early age, an important first step with a new class of any age will be to create some musical 'play' situations which will help to uncover the children's musical liveliness. Chapters 5 and 6 give suggestions for this.

The essentials in encouraging the development of children's music, then, are as follows:

- the child should be able to do, and recognize that s/he is doing, individual work in music and develop a sense of musical self;
- there should be opportunities for the child, as opposed to the teacher, to take musical control by bringing and developing initiatives and ideas about music;
- the child should be able to practise his/her own music, individually or with others.

The teaching style is important. It should be open to children's initiatives and interests, but should not rule out instruction in skills. Rowland (1984) provides a model which is especially appropriate for music. He calls this 'interpretative teaching' where the teacher or the child initiates, and there is a cycle in which the teacher's role is to reflect back, identify need and instruct. The control of learning is shared and passes between teacher and child. This model underlies the approaches to teaching which are described throughout this book.

Who teaches music?

Across the primary curriculum as a whole there has been an assumption that the class teacher is responsible for the education of the whole child and has a holistic view of a child's development. There has in the past been the view in primary education that music is 'different' in ways which mean that not all class teachers can or should tackle it, and the debates about specialist teaching continue (see also Chapter 2).

The crux of the matter is that music learning should be for the individual. This means:

- each child developing skills and understanding and the ability to use these musically in an independent way;
- music work being matched to each child's ability and needs;
- the teacher monitoring individual progress in music.

Only the class teacher is in a position to manage the time, space and resources which are necessary and to have a close enough knowledge of the child to make such learning possible. The question of who teaches music has a direct bearing therefore on what *kind* of curriculum music is available. If children are taught music only by a teacher other than their own, there are immediate limitations on what is possible and parts of the music curriculum, such as individual composition, may be left out altogether.

The proposal that individual children's learning in music should be overseen and monitored by the general class teacher does not imply that all learning situations should be individual ones, nor that children should never be taught by other teachers who may have particular musical skills. Children will, of course, do much of their musical activity with the whole class or in a group. A music specialist may take the class, especially at Key Stage 2, for development of particular singing or instrumental skills.

There are two additional important arguments in favour of the class teacher taking responsibility for music. The first is that attitudes to music are often strongly influenced by the ways in which provision for it is organized. If all the staff in a school take part in music and the teaching of it as they do in everything else, this carries the message that music is accessible to, and valued by, everyone. Where teaching is restricted to one or two staff, or worse still to someone coming in from outside, it is not surprising if pupils draw the conclusion that only some people can do music or that music-making depends on someone else being there to organize it. Such assumptions are carried into adult life and lie behind many teachers' lack of confidence in their own abilities to teach music, having still in mind the teaching models they grew up with.

The second argument goes back to the basic conception of music as intrinsically connected to everything else. A theme running through this book is that music is in many ways *the* great integrator of different aspects of human experience. This seems to be true both at the personal level, where music brings together the intellectual, physical, emotional and social dimensions in a powerful and holistic way, and across the broader fields of human understanding and action. Within the school setting music has an almost unique capacity for integrating aspects of different disciplines, since by its nature it has things in common with every other subject area. For teachers to be able fully to explore and exploit this they need to have management of the whole curriculum. This means more than just the inclusion of music in topic work, but rather the way in which music can contribute to other elements in the curriculum such as mathematics, science, language, literacy and movement. These are further explored in Chapter 8.

In recent music education debate the question of who should teach music has frequently been characterized as that of whether it should be the 'specialist' or the 'generalist', the generalist being any class teacher who is not a music specialist. The notion of labelling people as generalists or specialists is ill-conceived and can lead to an unhelpful polarization of roles. Many school staffs (or clusters of smaller schools) have several such music specialists among them, and a wide range of particular skills (instrumental, vocal, dance, technology, composing, appreciation) can be made available if everyone is willing to profess to them and to share them.

The approach taken here is that for the reasons given above the main responsibility for music in the curriculum must always rest with the class teacher. All specialist music skills in the school should be pooled and strategies found whereby these can be drawn on to benefit the widest range of children. To take responsibility for overall planning and resourcing, continuity and progression there should be in each school one *music co-ordinator* or subject leader, who may or may not be a specialist in the traditional sense. An important part of the co-ordinator's role will be to support colleagues. This is a complex undertaking, explored in some detail in Chapter 9.

The question of whether all class teachers have the ability to teach music is sometimes raised by class teachers themselves who feel inadequate both musically and in knowing what to teach. And it is also raised by those within the music profession and outside who take the view that music is essentially a specialism, simply not manageable by all. But extensive experience of teaching done by class teachers who have claimed to be incapable of it but who have received the support of either inservice courses or a co-ordinator in their school, or both, shows that specialist music skills are not essential to the provision of a good music curriculum. This is also supported by Mills (1991), who points out that there are alternative approaches to the same ends and that different schools can use the staff's combined skills in different ways. The findings of OFSTED music inspections during 1995–6 (Mills, 1997) show that:

> There is no evidence of a general link between 'specialist' teaching and the quality with which class music is taught in Key Stage 1 or Key Stage 2. Some specialists teach very effectively, but others do not.

It needs to be said at this point that having specialist skills can at worst lead to work which draws more on the teacher's musical ability than that of the children, sometimes to an extent seriously detrimental to pupils' development. Everyone has some musical skills which can be brought to bear on their class teaching. As Woodward *et al.* (1986) note, 'Everyone is somewhere on the musical map'. Nevertheless it is important to ask what abilities a class teacher needs in order to provide a rich and stimulating music curriculum. Broadly these are the musical abilities of an 'ordinary' adult who has recognized that s/he possesses such skills, brought together with a range of teaching skills which are transferable across the curriculum. The abilities required of the class teacher in handling music in the classroom are:

- to be a demonstrably careful, perceptive listener, responsive to sounds and to their qualities and to music;
- to use language confidently in a musical context;
- to have an imaginative approach to, and evident enthusiasm for, a wide variety of music, including children's own work;
- to investigate music with interest, using a range of skills for finding out about it;
- to be able to interact and communicate musically, however simple the level;
- to plan and provide for music learning of an ongoing kind within the whole curriculum for each child;
- to assess progress, identifying developmental needs and matching provision to them.

There is a widespread tendency to define 'musicality' in terms of the very specific skills of solo singing, the ability to play an instrument, or the ability to read music. Whilst these skills are obviously of value, much more to the point would be to consider the range of activities across which teachers can exercise the musical competence and responsiveness everyone has. It is crucial to recognize the teacher's role *as an ordinary adult* in initiating children into the practice of music.

Undoubtedly the most important aspect of how teachers display their musicality in the classroom is that of responsiveness to music as a listener. The children should see the teacher responding naturally to music, showing how anyone can become caught up in music and how it affects him or her. They can help children to reach through music's invisibility.

People experience music in very individual ways. Sometimes the feelings it arouses can be extremely intense:

> but that which did please me beyond anything in the world was the wind-musique when the angel comes down, which is so sweet that it ravished me, and indeed, in a word, did wrap up my soul so that it made me really sick, just as I have formerly been when in love with my wife; that neither then, nor all the evening going home, and at home, I was able to think of anything, but remained all night transported, so as I could not believe that ever any musique hath that real command over the soul of a man as did this upon me.
>
> (Samuel Pepys, *Diary*, 27 February 1668)

For some it may be difficult ever to hear music without wanting to dance, or jump about, or get up and get on with something physical. For some, music may be used as a means to calm and collectedness, a way of centring and finding a balance. And always it will depend on the music, or the time of day, or who one is with, and so on. Music 'hits' in different ways. All of which gives an alarming backdrop to the very idea of music being let loose inside a primary classroom. To what extent do teachers want their own inner responses called up in such a context? And how can they at one and the same time encourage sensitivity and real engagement for themselves and the children, whilst also containing the consequences of music's power?

Many adults describe themselves as 'non-musicians' or as 'unmusical', and hold their own musical capacities in very low regard. This may be partly because the yardstick they are using includes a list of technical performance skills, such as piano-playing. The poor musical self-esteem of some adults (Mills, 1991) can be traced to negative experiences from their own early education, such as rejection from the school choir. As a consequence, many primary teachers have little or no sense of musical self when considered in a teaching context. Yet this contrasts dramatically with the actual role of music in those same people's non-professional lives. For the benefit of the children it is of crucial importance that those who teach them do not bring into the classroom a negative musical self-image, but rather allow their real musical responsiveness and competence to show, and to evolve an effective teaching style on such a basis. Equally important is that those with specific performance skills use them in a sensitive and musical way. The worst of 'performance-phobia' is that it is infectious and can spread easily through a school, so that no one is able to take the risk of openly demonstrating musical skills and interests.

11

How can music be taught in the classroom?

Very often when a primary school is described as 'musical' this refers to a flourishing extra-curricular provision for choirs and instrumental groups, perhaps annual musical events such as Christmas concerts, shows or contributions to local festivals. In the wake of the 1988 Education Act this sort of musical activity is increasingly being seen by headteachers and governors as an important contribution in encouraging parents to choose to send children to the school. Until the introduction of National Curriculum music, it was not uncommon for such provision to represent almost the only music in a school, with some children receiving no teaching at all and many only a patchy experience offered more or less according to the teacher's inclination. In 1996 OFSTED were still finding considerable imbalances in the amount of teaching pupils received (OFSTED, 1996).

Extra-curricular provision, even where it includes large numbers of children and not just a chosen few, cannot be seen as more than a welcome extension to a properly organized and resourced provision for music as an integrated part of the whole curriculum for every child. For some schools and teachers this is still demanding considerable re-thinking of approaches to, and assumptions about, music.

So what are the practicalities of managing music within a primary classroom situation? The details of this are discussed in Chapters 5 and 6, but here some broad points are made in order to outline something of how the class teaching approach might work out in the day-to-day situation.

Learning in music requires an environment that stimulates pupils to be musically active and responsive, to develop their own skills and understanding, putting these to their own musical purposes, and above all to see music as a ready and accessible dimension of daily life. Time and resources must therefore be organized so that children can make and listen and move to music. Activities should take place individually, in small groups and as a class (DfEE, 1995) as part of daily classroom activity and not just once a week in an isolated slot. This applies to classes throughout the primary age-range.

The following are four general principles which might be discussed by a staff still in early stages of developing a full music curriculum:

- Work in music is essentially *practical* and involves children in first-hand experiences of singing and playing, moving and listening to their own and other people's music. Practical work needs space, time, organization and simple, good-quality equipment, stored or displayed so that it is directly accessible to the children within guidelines for use.

- *Listening* is the core musical skill. Children must be able to hear what they're doing. Teacher and class together should think about the classroom as a sound environment and find strategies for controlling sound, limiting noise, making quiet when it is needed, and planning sessions in which music can happen alongside other compatible activities. Support is needed at school management level for this.
- *Time* for music should be managed flexibly: two- to five-minute class times for songs, games/skill practice; twenty- to thirty-minute class sessions for listening and talking, review of group work, introducing music topics or ideas, skills instruction or learning new music; sequences of sessions of variable length for individual and small group work, initiated by the children, possibly commissioned by the teacher. In addition to blocked times for music, some of the ways of handling time are:
  - open access times for structured play/practice, tape-recording and IT/computer work;
  - listening to music as 'time-out' from words: for example, mid-session or at story-time;
  - music doubling with other things, e.g. movement, audible maths;
  - music to mark occasions: song choice for birthday or visit;
  - music as part of class management: singing the register, shoe-changing chants, games for lining-up times, special music for clearing away at the end of sessions.

  All these have their place. As in children's reading and writing, *frequency* is important; the once-a-week music lesson may play a part, but it is as inadequate in providing range of activity and opportunity as a once-a-week language slot would be.
- Music work should be *seen and heard*, displayed, collected and taken seriously. This requires display space with audio facility: for example, intermittent live presentations, tape player with headphones, music technology as well as visual support – explanations, photos, notation/scores and hands-on opportunities. Both individual and class work should be collected on cassette tape and children should have individual folios of their own work, contributing to building a music profile through the year.

In schools where music has been organized in such a way as to be isolated from the main curriculum, the above catalogue or requirements and resources may seem hard to envisage or even completely unrealistic in its demands. Obviously if this kind of organization is new it will take time to develop both strategies and resources. On the positive side, however, quite apart from being provision necessary to implement the National Curriculum for music, teachers who allow music to function fully in their classrooms like this find that the rewards are incalculable, not just in terms of music learning but of the impact it has on the class generally as a social group, their behaviour, general interest and motivation, ability to work together and confidence as individuals. In deep-level ways that are of the greatest importance to the well-being of all concerned, children and teacher, music can transform the life and work of a class.

The biggest initial step may be that of breaking the 'sound barrier'. For the children this involves becoming sensitive to the aural environment, learning to control sound and to ask for and make quiet with or for others. For the teacher it may involve an initial act of faith that this learning will happen quickly once the children understand that instruments and time for music will be regularly and frequently available (i.e. that the first time they use a 20-inch sizzle cymbal will not be the last) and that *noise*, which is quite unnecessary to music, both hurts and makes them feel bad.

The other daunting prospect may be that of finding *time* for a subject often treated as a low priority. Although time is always at a premium right across the primary curriculum, the problem of time for music dissolves to a considerable extent through good organization, by using the potentially time-wasting parts of the day just before lunch or play-times, and if the teacher understands and makes maximum use of the overlap between music and other areas, as discussed in Chapter 8.

Reviewing music in the school

Music is a whole-school matter. All staff need to be involved in teaching it. All staff need to be involved with children making it. All staff need to share a common understanding and attitude to music. Rooms, equipment and the sound environment should be managed on a whole-school basis. For music to be a quality experience for all children there must be regular review, by the whole staff of music throughout the school.

As part of any review of music in the school it is important that staff discuss the ethos of music in the school and the wider role it plays. Such a discussion might begin by considering the following aspects.

MUSIC AS A SUBJECT AREA IN ITS OWN RIGHT

This is how music is addressed within National Curriculum frameworks and how it must statutorily be provided for within the primary school.

Music is an art form with quite specific potential and skills and competencies and is an important part of the cultural heritage and living traditions of any people or social group. Each child's curriculum must introduce him/her to music in a wide variety of forms, as a discipline in its own right, and provide a progressive learning experience in performing, composing and listening to and appraising music. This is a process of initiation into a set of practices and the development of individual skills, creativity and response within those practices.

MUSIC CONTRIBUTING TO THE HEALTHY DEVELOPMENT OF THE CHILD

From the most ancient times and across all cultures the health-giving effects of music and musical activity have been acknowledged in different ways. The use of music as therapy for children and adults with special needs of many kinds is already widely developed. Continuous with this is the rapidly growing recognition of the value of music within the primary curriculum for the general development of all children. This becomes immediately obvious once children are involved in musical activity and that this often convinces the sceptical that they can't do without music in the classroom.

MUSIC AS A FORCE IN COMMUNITY LIFE

Music plays a part in the life of the school community parallel to that which it plays in the community at large. Music contributes to a group's sense of identity and to an individual's sense of belonging to a group. It is important that musical opportunities are open to all children, are balanced and presented in ways which are sensitive to differences of gender, race or religion. As a way of coming together, as a part of the ritual attaching to particular events, as a way of celebrating festivals and occasions or giving expression to group feeling, music performs an indispensable function. It also secures a balance of the aural with the other sensory aspects of a living environment, contributing thereby to a wholeness of approach.

MUSIC AS THE GREAT INTEGRATOR ACROSS THE CURRICULUM

Music by its nature holds extraordinary potential as a learning medium because of the shared ground and essential connectedness it has with each of the other subject areas. This potential has been little understood or exploited, mainly because, on the whole, music has been kept outside the rest of the primary curriculum. If it plays any part alongside other areas this is usually confined to a 'song about ...' whatever is the topic in

15

hand or 'creative music' loosely aimed at portraying the topic in hand. Yet music has *intrinsic* connections with everything else which offer ways in which ideas and experiences can be expressed or re-expressed, encountered in another form, explored in another medium, confirmed, reinforced, enriched and extended. These are all vital to ensuring that children's learning is more than superficial. (Chapter 8 sets out some ideas on this.)

In moving from a process of review towards making an action plan, the following ten questions may be useful:

1   What principles underlie the school's approach to music? How are equal opportunities addressed?
2   What music is going on in the school now? How do teachers and children currently perceive music? What changes need to be made?
3   What staff resources are available? What musical knowledge, interest and skills are available on the staff?
4   What changes to the class teaching arrangements does each teacher need to make?
5   What support do individual staff need?
6   How can each child's progression in music throughout the school be ensured?
7   How is children's musical development and attainment assessed and recorded?
8   How is accommodation for music managed?
9   What material resources are required?
10 How are *musical events* handled?

But in getting to know where people fundamentally are with music, all staff and all children might be asked to think about how they would complete the following:
'I am at my most musical when ... '

References

Blacking, J. (1976) *How Musical is Man?* London: Faber.
Britton, J. (1971) *Language and Learning.* Harmondsworth: Penguin.
DfEE (1995) *Music in the National Curriculum.* London: HMSO.
Mills, J. (1991) *Music in the Primary School.* Cambridge: CUP.
Mills, J. (1997) OFSTED Music Inspection Findings 1995–6. *Primary Music Today,* issue 8.
Nelson (1990) National Writing Project Series. Walton-on-Thames: Nelson.
OFSTED (1996) *Subjects and Standards.* London: HMSO.
Richardson, M. (1948) *Art and the Child.* London: University of London Press.

Rowland, S. (1984) *The Enquiring Classroom.* Lewes: Falmer Press.

Tough, Y. J. (1979) *Talk for Teaching and Learning.* London: Ward Lock Educational.

Wells, C. G. (1986) *The Meaning Makers.* London: Heinemann.

Wittgenstein, L. (1967) *Zettel.* Oxford: Blackwell.

Woodward, L., Mills, J. and Reynolds, W. (1986) *Primary Music in the UK: Generalists and Consultants.* Paper to Conference of United Kingdom Council for Music Education and Training, July 1986.

Music in Primary Schools: from the National Song Book to the National Curriculum
Stephen Ward

> The arts in the primary school need to be conceived of, and organized as, an integral part of every school day. The fact that one teacher is concerned with almost the whole of the child's daily curriculum makes this a possibility.
>
> (Gulbenkian Foundation, *The Arts in Schools*, 1982, p. 52)

Introduction

Chapter 1 asserts that everyone is musical, including teachers. The main message in this book is that, like all other subjects in the primary curriculum, music should be taught by the class teacher, supported by a subject co-ordinator. When the first edition was written in 1992, music could not be said to have been 'an integral part of the primary curriculum'. It was often taught exclusively by specialist teachers. In primary schools, the National Curriculum for music is now beginning to join the others as 'an integral part of every school day'. This is happening as more class teachers take on the role of teaching music to their children, supported by the music co-ordinator in the school, although there is still some way to go and many schools are still employing part-time specialized staff to take music lessons. This chapter will trace the development of music in primary schools and show how the National Curriculum has helped to change it from a subject taught mainly by music specialists to one which is taught by class teachers in the context of the primary curriculum. The evidence which exists about music in primary schools indicates that, before the advent of the National Curriculum, it had *not* been an integral part of the school day. Music tended to be seen as a 'specialist' subject, taught by the music specialist and often relegated to the 'extra-curricular' times of the day for exclusive groups of children. Other subjects, including children's visual art, became part of the texture of the primary curriculum with exciting and imaginative learning activities for individuals, groups and the class under the general guidance of the class teacher.

HMI and OFSTED are the only source of detailed assessment of the provision of music in primary schools. The HMI National Survey of Primary Education (DES, 1978, paras 5.96–5.104) found that children's main experience of music was through class singing. For some children there was listening to recorded music and some playing of percussion instruments to accompany the singing. There was, however, very little experimental work for children and composition was rare. In subsequent inspections during the 1980s HMI found a very wide range in the quality and extent of provision in music for children; they identified approximately 10 per cent of schools which offered 'good practice' (DES, 1991a, 1991b). While there were small pockets of good practice in which there was a range of musical activities for children, it was singing in large groups which was the staple diet of the music curriculum and many children got little else. There was likely to be some music listening, mostly in school assemblies, and some use of percussion instruments in class work. Other instrumental playing would be recorder groups and orchestral instrument playing. However, these were invariably on an extra-curricular basis at lunchtimes and after school and for self-selected groups of children, usually girls.

Another of HMI's findings was that music, usually class singing, was often well done by specialist music teachers, and that the quality of children's musical experience was determined by 'the teacher's competence *as a musician*' (DES, 1978, para. 5.104, my italics). This tendency for the quality of music teaching to be dependent on the teacher as an 'expert' in the subject is unusual in the primary curriculum. For example, it would be surprising if HMI were to find that primary children's learning in mathematics should be determined by their teacher's competence *as a mathematician*. Music found itself a special place in the primary curriculum as an exclusive and inaccessible area of knowledge and expertise for teachers, unique in often being seen as a subject which can only be delivered by an expert. The emphasis was on the musical *product* which was performed in the school, rather than the children's musical *learning*.

The 1980s saw rapid developments in the role of the curriculum co-ordinator across a range of subjects (see Alexander, 1984, p. 188). However, music is the one subject which was left out of this pattern of generalist teaching in the primary school and the marginalization of music into the curriculum backwater of specialist music teaching had starved it of many of the exciting developments which occurred in, for example, language, writing, mathematics, science, art and humanities. Why, then, did music retain this exclusively specialist form of teaching and narrow range of activities within the primary school?

The origins of primary music education

What is now known as state-maintained primary education may be said to have begun around 1870 with the Education Act which made elementary schooling compulsory for all children. This period of schooling was characterized by a narrow 'three Rs' curriculum taught from the front in a didactic way to large classes of 50 or more. Music fitted into this model of teaching and learning by the class becoming a unison chorus to the piano accompaniment of the teacher. The teacher's specialist contribution to the children's musical education would be the ability to play the piano and to be able to detect whether the singing was in tune. The emphasis was on *performance*. The children were a chorus to be directed into accurate production of songs, probably from *The National Song Book* and *The New National Hymn Book*, which would fulfil the following functions:

- choral accompaniment to the collective worship in the school religious service;
- strengthening the corporate sense of class and school identity;
- strengthening a sense of nationalism through patriotic songs.

The Plowden Report (1967) refers to these early examples of vocal music teaching, describing them as 'well done' where the teacher was 'musically educated'. However,

> in a great number of schools where no such teacher was to be found, standards were low. Out-of-tune and sometimes broken pianofortes and wheezy harmoniums were beyond the skill of even the most musically gifted to use well; but far too often, even if the instrument was satisfactory, the playing was wretched and the choice of music deplorable ... (p. 251)

Hoggart (1957) describes the choral singing in the Church tradition as a strong part of nineteenth- and early twentieth-century life among the urban working class; so too was the singing of popular songs to piano accompaniment in public houses and clubs. Another important facet of musical life among the working class was singing to piano accompaniment in the home. The commitment of the financial resources of urban working families to such a piano would be considerable at that time and demonstrates a great reverence for the instrument itself. Wood (1991, p. 1) writes from his working-class childhood experiences of 'keeping up with the Joneses' in Leeds:

> Joe and Sarah were sitting in front of their cosy coal fire having a 'chin-wag' one Friday night after a hard day's work. . . . Sarah cleared her throat and, with slight trepidation, said, 'Joe, does tha think we can afford a pianna?' Joe took his pipe out of his mouth and replied, 'Nay lass, what use would a pianna be to us? Noan on us can play one.'
> 'Well, Joe,' said Sarah, 'them next door 'ave got one, and them at t'bottom 'ouse are 'avin' one delivered tomorra.' After a lengthy argument it was

agreed that Joe would go into Leeds on Saturday afternoon to see about a 'pianna'.

A combination of reverence for the piano and of respect for those 'musical' people who could play it are fundamental to the traditions of music teaching in Britain. Playing the piano was the sign of musical specialism and it was translated into practice through accompanied singing. In asking for a teacher with musical expertise, schools would invariably advertise 'ability to play the piano essential'. The predominance of piano-playing as the single token of musical expertise or experience lived on to limit the musical potential of children. Children who were not 'musical' were limited to singing to the piano accompaniment with little opportunity for them to listen to their own voice production.

The limitations of this model were attacked as early as 1908 by Macpherson (Rainbow, 1984, p. 6), who had noticed that there was singing and piano playing but no listening:

> The first thing that strikes me as singularly and lamentably deficient in the present state of music-teaching is the cultivation of the child's ear. Little or nothing is done in this direction ... and, although the eye is trained daily in countless ways, the sensitiveness of the ear is allowed to remain undeveloped until its power of discernment becomes atrophied, and finally, for all practical purposes, ceases to exist.

Another aspect of musical culture was that of *audience appreciation*. It will be shown below that this 'cultural heritage' view of music education is still prevalent and played a significant role in determining the National Curriculum for music. This reverence for 'serious' music, which can only be really appreciated by 'the musical', and a veneration for the 'musically gifted' in the form of the teacher-pianist were largely responsible for creating the music curriculum in elementary schools and later in primary schools.

Developments in teaching and learning in primary music

Modern primary schools have come a long way in shaking off the Victorian image. Now parents are welcome into schools; windows let in light and children engage in a wide range of different learning activities across the curriculum. However, the predominantly 'performance' role of music in the primary school has continued. Music still plays a sanctifying role in school assemblies and HMI noted in 1991 that the main element of school music for most children was the class singing lesson or hymn practice (DES, 1991a). Why was the progress made in other aspects of the primary school so limited in music?

The Plowden Report (1967) was a watershed for primary education and gave a national voice to 'child-centred' primary education. Briefly, Plowden recommended that learning should take place through the child's engaging in activities; children should be helped to gain control of their own learning and not always be passive in teacher-directed learning situations. This meant that children should be able to learn from each other by working on activities in groups, and that children should be able to interact on an individual and group basis with the teacher. Further, children should be encouraged to learn independently, should be allowed some choice of activity and to be able to work in areas of interest. But class teaching was not excluded (para. 756):

> Choral singing, games and physical education for the older children are obvious examples of things taught to a whole class. Experiences like listening to a story, a poem, or music may be heightened by being shared with a class, but it is often best to leave children to make their private and individual response. There are no infallible rules.... . Class teaching for these various purposes is sensible and helps to make the class a unity. On the other hand, the practice of setting a whole class laboriously to copy notes from a blackboard, and other similar mass drills are best avoided.

It was not that the class should never sing together, but that other learning situations for children's musical learning are required. Plowden notes (para. 692a) that the teaching of music, even in the early 1960s, was different from other subjects in its methods:

> In many schools mass instruction is given in music, and in music alone, to a whole class or even combined classes: little is attempted in groups or by individual methods, and teacher direction persists in this field even in schools where it has almost disappeared in language, mathematics and art. Massed hymn practice and massed festival songs sometimes dominate the scene in both infant and junior schools, and the musical merits of teachers tend to be judged on the basis of their capacity to direct, and accompany on the piano, such choral activities.

A key notion underlying the Plowden model of teaching and learning was that of the child's individual development from his/her own starting point, rather than the imposition of 'knowledge from without'. Again Plowden says of music (para. 692b):

> The principle of individual progression is seldom consistently and successfully carried into the musical sphere. In schools where progress in language is carefully checked, the achievements expected in music of older pupils as compared with the younger ones are often ill-defined and vary enormously from school to school.

Throughout the 1970s, in response to Plowden, so-called 'progressive' primary education got under way. Classrooms came to be arranged with desks in groups and the class lesson, in many schools, became just one in a repertoire of the teacher's forms of interaction with children, along with group and individual work. However, research into primary classrooms during the late 1970s and early 1980s found, in reality, a wide range of different models of teaching. For example, HMI (DES, 1978), Galton, Simon and Croll (1980) and Mortimore *et al.* (1988) found that teachers' organizational practice greatly varied between four types:

- Class teaching with individual work;
- Children organized to work in groups;
- Individualized learning with little class work;
- A mixture of these.

The same research also demonstrated the myth of progressive education in British primary schools (Simon, 1981). Although the children were found to be *sitting* in groups, group work in which children interacted together on task-related activities rarely took place. Very few children were engaged in *discovery learning* activities along the lines suggested by Plowden (DES, 1978). The most consistent change in the pattern of teaching and learning was the move towards individualized learning in which children worked on individual programmes, often from commercially produced materials, with the teacher attempting to interact separately with individual children. The result of this was that some teachers spent little productive time with children because attention was so diffused among members of the class (Galton, Simon and Croll, 1980). It was here that Plowden's recommendations seem to have gone wrong as teachers interpreted children's 'individual progression' to mean that they should learn and be taught *individually*.

Bennett and Dunne (1992) argue that the attention which teachers should give is in setting learning tasks for children which move from the child as an individual learner to the child as a social learner. They show that the quality of children's interaction and learning in groups is critically dependent on the kind of task which they are set:

> The message is clear. Individualization, based on the notion of the child as a 'lone scientist', needs balancing with a pedagogy which allows the child to take on the role of a 'social being' in a move from individualists to co-operative classroom endeavours. (p. 17)

However, in music there was never even a *myth* about progressivism. It was as though Plowden passed music by. Edwards and Mercer (1987) found that teachers were committed to a Plowden ideology and methodology if they only had the means to bring it about. For music education, though, there was often not even an intention to bring music into an integrated classroom and, to some extent, the organizational problems meant that music was experienced largely through the class lesson. Whereas art, literacy, science and mathematics lent themselves readily to independent group and individual learning activities, music appeared less easy to organize in this way. (Chapters 5 and 6 in this book show how such activities can be organized in music.) The *performance* emphasis in schools also meant that the teacher was often rehearsing children for some production; if no production was in sight, then the rehearsal model still prevailed. The concept of teachers focusing on *children's* own learning in music towards their independence across a breadth of skills was often completely missing.

Specialist music teachers and music co-ordinators

The two main reasons for the exploratory learning model of music not taking place in the primary classroom were the cultural tradition of the piano-led 'performance paradigm' and the organizational difficulties in the classroom. However, a further reason why these difficulties were not overcome was that music teaching was seen as the role of the specialist teacher. The result of this was that class teachers did not integrate music into their class work with children; there was little grasp among 'non-specialist' class teachers of what children were supposed to be learning and, therefore, no means of judging and assessing their learning.

In the primary school all subjects in the curriculum, apart from music, have been taught by the class teacher. The virtues of the generalist class teacher are worth remembering: when a single teacher is responsible for the whole of the child's education for a year s/he can assess progression for the individual and compare relative strengths and weaknesses in different subjects or activities. This overview of the child's progress enables the teacher to match appropriate activities to the child's level and to monitor learning with sensitivity.

During the 1960s and 1970s the music specialist's role became firmly established and the class or school singing session became part of the organizational structure of the school. The music specialist would exchange classes with other teachers to take their music, or would often take the whole school for singing or for hymn practice. This would be a time when the class teachers might be free for a brief spell to do other activities such as clearing up on Friday afternoons, hearing readers, dealing with special needs learners. Frequently the music specialist was given additional remuneration and status in the form of a graded post. At that time, music was likely to be one of the few, if not the only, subject to attract additional staff funding in this way; it was done, of course, to attract the rare commodity of the pianist who could handle singing in its variously needed forms: assemblies, carol service, concerts for parents. HMI (DES, 1978) found that 70 per cent of schools had a teacher with curriculum responsibility for music, while only 51 per cent had a post for language and only 17 per cent for science. This seems paradoxical given that music was usually low in a teacher's curriculum priorities (Ashton *et al.*, 1975). Alexander (1984, p. 189) explains this by showing that the offering of graded posts for music was acceptable to other teachers because

> the child's musical development and awareness are seen as outside the defined zone of the competence of the class teacher, to allocate posts of responsibility for music, as for 'display' or 'stock', threatens nobody's professional self-esteem.

Yet even during the 1960s Plowden (1967) was critical of the specialist approach to teaching music and identified the lack of musical education of the class teacher as a problem (p. 252, para. 690):

> Comparatively few primary schools ... can, for some time to come, expect to have a music specialist as a full-time member of the staff and it is even doubtful whether a specialist responsible for most of the teaching is desirable. It is the musical education of the non-specialist which, in our view, is the key to the problem.

So it was Plowden who pointed out the need for enabling class teachers to teach classroom music and that the way to do this is through their 'musical education'. What such an education needs to consist of is examined in Chapter 9. However, it was not until the 1980s that any attempt was made to develop the role of the *music co-ordinator*, rather than *specialist teacher*.

Before the National Curriculum, then, music in primary schools tended to be a narrow provision of singing by the whole class to the piano, taught by the music specialist, with some instrumental tuition for the 'musically gifted'. It was taught mainly by specialist teachers who often concentrated their efforts on performance for public display to parents. Well-performed mass singing and instrumental playing still played its Victorian role of demonstrating publicly the corporate quality of the school, and headteachers put pressure on their music specialists to deliver this in the interest of the school's image in the community.

Just as many class teachers perceived themselves as musically incapable, so they saw children as musically either gifted or ungifted. Music was, therefore, seen as a subject to be taken seriously only by the few. The majority were seen as voices to swell the singing with real achievement, restricted to the musically gifted or inclined. What was needed was a music curriculum which would hand teaching over to the class teacher

25

and hand the musical learning over to children – all children – so that they could engage in musical activities, as they had engaged in artistic ones. In this way, music could take its place alongside the rest of the primary curriculum, taught by the class teacher who is, in turn, supported by the music curriculum co-ordinator. In 1990 it remained to be seen whether the National Curriculum for music would be one that could be taught by class teachers, or would be an elitist curriculum for the 'musically able' to be taught by the music specialist. Any doubts were dispelled by the National Curriculum Music Working Group who, in their final report (DES and Welsh Office, 1991b, p. 61), specified that

> In primary schools, the music curriculum will in the main be delivered by general class teachers.

The National Curriculum for music: professional practice and political debates

Music, along with art and physical education, was one of the last of the National Curriculum subjects to be set in place. This was, of course, an indication of its low priority for the government. Indeed, there is an apocryphal story that the prime minister at the time, Margaret Thatcher, with a casual stroke of the pen, deleted music from the list of proposed subjects, and that it was only reinstated by the Secretary of State for Education, Kenneth Baker, following his attendance at an inspirational schools music concert in London. However, despite its low status, the National Curriculum for music did have a remarkable, and highly publicized, journey through the processes of consultation and approval and the story is worth telling for what it reveals about the public perceptions, and the politics of, music education.

The National Curriculum was formed through the process of a combination of expert advice and consultation with the teaching profession and the public. A working group of specialists for each of the ten subjects made proposals for Attainment Targets and Programmes of Study, which were then made public for consultation before the Secretary of State for Education decided on the content of the Statutory Orders.

In the early part of 1991 the world of music education awaited the first interim report of the National Curriculum Music Working Group (DES and Welsh Office, 1991a). It is reasonable to say that most of the others in the world of primary education were *not* waiting for it. By this time there had already been an avalanche of National Curriculum documents in eight curriculum areas and Year 2 teachers were anticipating their first copies of national tests, the Standard Assessment Tasks, to be administered in the first half of the coming summer term. Probably little was further from the minds of most primary teachers than proposals for a statutory music curriculum. However, its arrival was greeted with some warmth by those who were interested in developments in primary music education. In the first version of the National Curriculum, Attainment Targets were grouped under headings of Profile Components.* It proposed two Profile Components, each with two attainment targets:

PC1	Making Music	AT1	Performing
		AT2	Composing
PC2	Understanding Music	AT3	Listening
		AT4	Knowing

This structure was consistent with the developments which had already taken place in secondary GCSE music. The placing of 'performing' and 'composing' as separate attainment targets was to establish active children's music-making throughout the 5–16 curriculum. These signalled the prospect of making the primary music curriculum, like art and writing, much more a medium for children's original expression, as the Working Group pointed out:

> Composing should include exploring sounds – for example, those made by the body, the face, and everyday objects and instruments, including keyboards and computers as well as more conventional instruments. Exploration can be gradually extended and developed to include inventing rhythmic and melodic patterns, improvising ... composing ... and arranging own songs or other pieces of music.
>
> (DES and Welsh Office, 1991a, p. 14)

Simply 'listening with reverence' was to be replaced by listening activities which are linked to children's own music-making and composition:

> Listening to music has traditionally featured in the school music curriculum. We wish to extend the range of listening in a way that will help pupils to become better performers and composers ... (*ibid.*)

So the National Curriculum was to provide the opening of the music curriculum to a broader range of activities enabling children to become active in the making and learning process. The Secretary of State for Education at this time was Kenneth Clarke. His response to the proposed attainment target structure was that it was too complex and did not reflect the pattern which had been used in the art and physical education proposals. Therefore, the Working Group was instructed to revert to just three attainment targets, not grouped under profile components. There

---

* In the first version of the National Curriculum, attainment targets were grouped under headings of profile components. Profile components have since been dropped.

27

was, even at this time, an awareness that the National Curriculum was becoming too complex and it was part of Clarke's expressed intention of making it more simple and comprehensible to the general public. It also reflected, of course, a government view, highlighted by Robinson (1991), that arts subjects are less important than other subjects which are linguistic or technological. This lower status was also reflected in the fact that, while there are statutory statements of attainment at the end of each key stage, the statements of attainment at each of the ten levels are *non-statutory* and, therefore, optional.

It is important to understand the way in which the National Curriculum came about in practice. The working groups in all subjects were called upon to produce their proposals very rapidly and with limited resources (Coulby, 1996, p. 9). The effect of this was that the groups were forced to rely upon the current expertise of the membership, with little opportunity to examine practice in schools. Much of the original National Curriculum was constructed by hard-pressed professionals during weekends in hotels. However, the effect of current 'good practice' in school was important. The National Curriculum had to be a balance between what was already being done in schools and what *ought* to be done. The working groups in all the subjects had to be heavily dependent on current practice if they were to propose something which was to be attainable in schools. In the English proposals (DES and Welsh Office, 1988), for example, the Working Group drew heavily on the developing practice in primary schools in children's writing with the work of the National Writing Project and the use of meaningful approaches to the teaching of reading, drawing on the work of Smith (1978) and Waterland (1985) for example. Brian Cox, the chair of the English Working Group, gives a good account of the influences on the group's proposals (Cox, 1991).

The Music Working Group was under similar pressure of time and had little opportunity to examine practice for themselves. What is more, there was little direct input from those with primary knowledge and expertise. The membership included only one representative from a primary school: a teacher in charge of an infants department who had a particular interest in music education. There appeared to be little other awareness of learning in the primary curriculum context and the primary voice was probably marginalized. Also, while the group was able to draw upon examples of good practice in singing, as shown above, current practice in most primary schools was very varied in both breadth and quality. Despite developments over the previous thirty years of practical classroom approaches such as those of Orff and Kodaly followed by composition work growing alongside that pioneered in secondary schools (for example, through the Schools Council Project led by John Paynter), there existed no widespread or agreed models of well-developed composition work. So the parallels in English of children's original writing simply did not exist. The group drew on the experience of HMI and, as they state about primary schools in their interim document (DES and Welsh Office, 1991a, p. 5):

> The least well developed aspect of the work seen was composing. Only a few schools were giving sufficient attention to enabling children to explore the properties of sound, experimenting with rhythmic and melodic patterns and creating their own compositions.

So, as there was no healthy model of children's composition in existence in primary schools, composition secured its place in the music National Curriculum through the successful secondary school experience of GCSE music courses. Therefore, there was little evidence of the understanding of the developmental approach to learning which informed the English National Curriculum document with its emphasis on reading from meaningful material and children's emergent writing. The attainment targets of Performing and Composing could only be based on rather hazy notions of what children might manage and at the consultation stages little notice was taken of contributions from those who had researched the field of young children's composition.

The Secretary of State, supported by other right-wing ideologues, challenged the Music Working Group's notion of music as a practical subject for children and introduced an additional pressure of the need for knowledge and understanding of the repertoire, history and traditions of music:

> I find it difficult to see how the framework you are proposing, based on your view of music as essentially a practical study, will encourage and allow such pupils to develop their knowledge and understanding of the repertoire, history and traditions of music.

(DES and Welsh Office, 1991a, para. 8)

The view of the music curriculum which underlies Clarke's statement is of music as something which the cultured and educated person should *know about*, but not actually take part in; it is knowing about the music of others; it is not about making music and not about music as something which everyone can be involved in making; nor does it acknowledge the role for children of making music as a way of gaining understanding of it. Again, it is the view that music is a part of the *cultural heritage*, to be revered, but not part of everyday life; the making of music should be restricted to elite 'musical people', rather than be an activity in which anyone may engage. This was a part of the attempt by the Secretary of

State to revert to a curriculum in which the child is to be made the recipient of 'knowledge', rather than an active participant in the learning process. It was made clear in Clarke's Statement on Primary Education which he made at the time (DES, 1991c) and it was reflected in the response of a right-wing lobby which criticized the interim proposals for suggesting that pupils could study rock music and electronic music, rather than being presented with the knowledge of Western classical music:

> On this curriculum, pupils will be able to study music for 10 years without gaining a sound knowledge of either the history or the techniques of Western classical music, which is surely one of the greatest achievements of our civilization.

> (O'Hear, 1991)

The Working Group later protested that their intention was that pupils should experience a variety of music, not that they should experience *no* Western classical music. They had, in fact, specified a number of musical techniques which were heavily Western orientated. However, more disturbing for this writer was the suggestion that pupils might be led away from an appreciation of the differences in musical worth. O'Hear (*ibid.*) was concerned that the Working Group's definition of music

> admits the heavy metal rocker, belting out his crude rhythms and anarchistic messages at 125 dB into the company of Beethoven, Schumann, Brahms, Duke Ellington and Leonard Bernstein.

The irony of this is that O'Hear's predecessors, as critics of this 'cultural relativism', would almost certainly have recoiled from the notion of Beethoven and Duke Ellington appearing in the same list of recommendations. Of course, O'Hear's criticisms are born of twin assumptions about the absolute and immutable artistic quality of certain works and that education is about the cultural transmission of these works to the young, regardless of pupils' own interests and tastes. This 'cultural heritage' model of music as that to be 'heard and respected' was to be offered to primary school children.

Of course, the 'rock versus the classics' debate centres on secondary schools. For primary schools the question of *which* music children should listen to and appraise is different. It is interesting to note that the great majority of the music which children are asked to listen to is music written for adults. Whereas huge numbers of songs continue to be written for children to sing, there is a tiny strand of music which has been written specifically for children's listening. This is to be contrasted with the colossal growth of high-quality children's literature which has flourished and which the English National Curriculum Working Group (DES and

Welsh Office, 1988) was able to draw upon and recommend for primary schools. The issue in music for primary schools, then, is less whether music for children is 'culturally acceptable', and more to do with which parts of adult music can be relevant to children.

There was wide consultation on the Interim Report. In their revised proposals published in August (DES and Welsh Office, 1991b) the Working Group responded to the request for simplicity by reducing the Attainment Targets to three:

    AT1   Performing
    AT2   Composing
    AT3   Appraising

It was gratifying to see that the Working Group, while bowing to the request for simplicity, had not moved from the intention to make music a practical subject and, in particular, had preserved an Attainment Target for Composition, a cornerstone of musical activities for children.

'Appraising Music' was to include both listening to music and having a knowledge of it. This was the concession to the 'cultural heritage' view of music in the Chair's letter to the Secretary of State:

> We have ... designed the third attainment target, 'Appraising' having very much in mind your concern for pupils' need to develop a knowledge and understanding of the repertoire, history and traditions of music. (p. vi)

However, the Working Group retained their position on music as a practical subject:

> There was a tremendously high level of support for our basic approach to the design of a music curriculum and, in particular, for our conviction that music is essentially a practical study ... (p. vi)

This 'reduced weight' model generally found acceptance among the professional music world because it kept a balance of two to one with the 'active' elements: Performing and Composing.

Next came the publication in January 1992 of the proposals of the National Curriculum Council (NCC, 1992). This stage in the process for all subjects was when the NCC acted as a kind of arbiter to make a new set of proposals balancing all views expressed about the Working Group's proposals. While the document was entitled 'a Report to the Secretary of State', in fact the recommendations also incorporated the Secretary of State's own views. The extent to which the NCC proposal diverged from the Working Group's recommendations was an indication of the extent to which the proposals had been accepted by politicians and other non-professionals. In other subjects, notably English and History, the publication of the NCC Report had been the point at which the conflict of views between professionals and politicians had been exposed. Music was an extreme case of the professional and political differences and the NCC Report recommended a further slimming down of the Attainment Targets from three to two:

AT1   Performing and Composing: The development of the ability to perform and compose music.

AT2   Knowledge and Understanding: The development of knowledge and understanding of musical history and theory, including the ability to listen to and appraise music.

The rationale given for this change was the need for further simplicity, for coherence and to bring music into line with art and physical education with just two attainment targets each. It was argued (NCC, 1992, p. 14) that:

> the four strands of the music curriculum – performing and composing, knowledge and understanding – fall logically into two categories, the one focusing on the development of the theoretical understanding and historical knowledge. The two AT approach reflects this logic in an easily intelligible way.

The Music Working Group's model in which music is predominantly *an activity* was substantially damaged by this and transformed into one which is much more concerned with *knowing about* music. The professional outcry against this was well expressed by Swanwick in a letter to the *Times Educational Supplement* (24 January 1992):

> The major impediment to professional acceptance of the report is the implication in the attainment targets that knowledge and understanding is essentially tied up with knowing *about* music and does not enter into performing and composing. This may not have been intended but it is inescapable in the way that the attainment targets are defined. Furthermore, the balance has been tipped heavily towards factual knowledge *about* music rather than knowledge *of* music by the actual working of the second attainment target (composing). This will increase the amount of factual information within a subject which is already restricted to a small corner of time in the school curriculum.

The implications for primary music were especially dispiriting for those who had seen music developing as an expressive mode for children growing up in a multicultural society. That children should learn the chronology of seven periods of Western musical history was seen to be highly inappropriate and based on a crude notion of history which was not shared by the History National Curriculum orders. The examples given in the programmes of study caused particular disquiet, indicating that its authors were out of touch with all recent developments in music education. Examples for listening were drawn from the Western classical tradition and were almost all of a programmatic type (Beethoven's *Pastoral Symphony*, Saint Saëns' *Carnival of the Animals*). There were no examples from women composers and there were a number of perplexing items, for example, that children at Key Stage 2 should 'comment on distinctive musical elements in a Bach Fugue' (NCC, 1992, p. 27).

While acknowledging the importance of composition and performance of music, the NCC had obviously found the need to respond to the criticisms of O'Hear and others in making a culturally prescriptive curriculum based on a traditional music curriculum and to include elements of a traditional 'appreciation' model taught by specialists.

In order to understand the reason for this it is important to be aware of the wider political context in which the consultations about the music curriculum were taking place. The debate about music was a continuation of the debate which ran through the National Curriculum from the beginning. It was a conflict between professional members of the Working Groups and the political voices at the then Department of Education and Science. Blenkin and Kelly (1981) show how two opposing views of the nature of knowledge prevailed at the DES: one was the professional view of the curriculum as learning processes, the other was the lay view of knowledge as factual content which can be transmitted to others in subject packages. This political tension was lived out in the National Curriculum debates concerning the core curriculum subjects during 1989 and 1990 (Ward, 1996). It began with the Secretary of State's conflict with the Mathematics Working Group about the application of mathematics as against number facts; it continued in the Science Working Party with the Secretary of State's rejection of the proposed attainment targets for exploration and communication in science which had to be combined into the attainment targets for knowledge and understanding (Ritchie, 1996). As shown above, the Secretary of State expressed serious misgivings about 'music as a practical subject'. This was the musical version of the old theme: knowledge cannot be seen as a process in which to engage – 'doing music'. Knowledge was seen exclusively as facts to be learned and stored. In terms of music, this had to mean learning about composers, their works, their dates as a kind of branch of history. Practical music was seen as exclusively for the 'musical' and the 'gifted' and not to be the entitlement of all children.

The National Curriculum legislation had been drawn up at the beginning of the government's third term of office in 1987–8. The first subjects had been implemented during the middle of this period. Music, as one of the last three, was being discussed at a point a few months away from a general election in which education was made a key political issue.

At this time the Secretary of State was urging a *back to basics* approach to primary schools, both in emphasis on the three Rs and in his criticisms of 'progressive' teaching methods (DES, 1991d) as part of the 'simple, traditionalist' approach to education which was the platform on which the Conservative Party was fighting the 1992 election campaign. It was important, then, for the Secretary of State to be able to argue publicly that he was *standing up to woolly and idealistic professionals* who sought to make the curriculum too complex and to prevent children from acquiring 'real knowledge'. In fact, it appears that the Secretary of State had underestimated not only the intensity of discontent among the professional music educators, but also the extent of their allegiances outside the education sphere, and the next stage in the National Curriculum process was quite extraordinary.

For all the other subjects the proposals in the NCC's report had proceeded smoothly to be adopted as the draft and final orders, to become statute. But this was not to be so for music. The first surprise was that the chairs of the Working Groups for both art and music 'broke ranks' and publicly criticized the National Curriculum Council proposals for their over-emphasis on *knowledge about* the subjects. This had never happened before. Even Brian Cox, the chair of the English Working Group, who since has made known his disagreements with the Secretary of State (Cox, 1991), made no public statement at the time of the consultations. The second surprise was that the Curriculum Council for Wales announced its full acceptance of the proposals of the Music Working Group, bringing it into opposition with the NCC. Formerly the agreement between NCC and the CCW had been taken for granted. But the music proposals brought the two Councils into open conflict, with the prospect of a different curriculum for music in England and Wales. A third significant event was the response of large numbers of celebrities from musical performance. These included the highly acclaimed conductor, Sir Simon Rattle, who, at the beginning of his concerts throughout January 1992, announced his criticisms to the audience and invited them to write to their members of parliament to express opposition to the NCC proposals.

Clarke responded, dodging artfully between the factions. It was a historic first that the draft orders, for both art and music (DES, 1992), which were published at the end of January differed from the NCC proposal. The draft orders still specified just two Attainment Targets:

AT1 Performing and Composing: The ability to perform and compose music with understanding.

AT2 Listening and Appraising: The development of the ability to listen to and appraise music, including knowledge of musical history.

However, in a climb-down from the emphasis on knowledge, it was specified that AT1 should occupy *two-thirds of the time*, as against one-third on AT2. This restored the emphasis on practical activity in music and, in the crude terms of amount of time spent on the subject, it was tantamount to restoring Performing and Composing as separate attainment targets. There was a significant reference to 'understanding' within the performing and composing, again a concession to the critics of the 'knowledge/practical' divide. It also restored 'listening and appraising', which had been the Working Group's original terminology, for AT2 and reference to 'knowledge' was gone.

But the music education world was still not satisfied and the United Kingdom Council for Music Education and Training met once more to launch a further offensive at the last consultation stage before the draft orders were confirmed. This time international celebrities joined the fray and the French composer and conductor, Pierre Boulez, pointed out in the *Guardian* (17 February 1992) that:

> To expect all children by the age of 11 to understand the distinctive characteristics of medieval, renaissance, romantic, recent and contemporary music is totally unrealistic. To require by law that every 14-year-old in the land shall study symphony and oratorio is ludicrously arbitrary.

This was all the more ironical considering that the Secretary of State had, just before, sung the praises of traditionalist approaches reported by HMI in their study of French primary schools (DES, 1991d).

The CCW went on to produce a separate set of draft and final orders which were identical to the Working Group's proposal. This gave an embarrassing legitimacy to the Working Group at the expense of the Secretary of State. And it meant that music in Wales could be different from music in England. There had been differences in the National Curriculum between English and Welsh schools, but these had always been about Welsh matters: Welsh language, history and geography. The differences in music revealed for the first time in the history of the National Curriculum ideological disagreements about the fundamental principles of a subject.

The 1995 Dearing revision of the National Curriculum

The summer of 1993 found the National Curriculum and its assessment machinery in disarray. The then Secretary of State, John Patten, had pursued a confrontational stance against professionals and continued to insist upon high levels of statutory testing. This, together with the burden of the overloaded statutory curriculum, had eventually brought teachers to unprecedented industrial action. Such a state of affairs resulting from the hasty and chaotic introduction of the National Curriculum with its compound political and professional agenda had been predicted by commentators from the beginning (see Coulby, 1996). With Patten sick at home for the summer, and his Minister, Lady Emily Blatch, in charge, the government yielded to the teachers and set up a review of the whole National Curriculum and its assessment under the Chair of Sir Ron Dearing. Dearing's task was to recommend a slimmed-down curriculum, giving teachers more control over the time and content, and to produce a manageable form of assessment.

As for all the other subjects, the Music Working Group was re-assembled to revise the curriculum for music. The changes they made proved to be uncontentious. The 'slimming' process in the case of music left a slight document with very little specified content. In the light of this the Working Group found the need to publish a separate, commercially produced document in which they were able to outline their thinking and make further recommendations for teachers (Pratt and Stephens, 1995).

Effectively, there was no change to the statutory curriculum. Instead there was simplification, tidying up and some changes of emphasis rather than content. The same two Attainment Targets (Performing and Composing, Listening and Appraising) were maintained. Interestingly, the three Attainment Targets for Wales (Performing, Composing and Appraising) preserved the differences between the Welsh and English versions. The fact that Pratt and Stephens do not comment on this suggests that the tensions and differences had been buried, rather than resolved. The Programmes of Study are not specified under Attainment Targets. This was intended to allow the three elements of music – performing, composing and listening – to be 'integrated holistically, each affecting and influencing each other' (Pratt and Stephens, 1995, p. 5). There was greater encouragement for Listening and Appraising to be seen as core skills running through all musical activity and for the musical elements (of timbre, pitch, duration and so on) to be a focus for learning across both ATs. The Programmes of Study were grouped into six broad strands and spelled out in much less detail, leaving teachers freedom of interpretation and emphasis.

Progress in teaching and learning since the National Curriculum

Despite the difficulties which teachers had experienced with the National Curriculum overall, it would appear that the implementation of the primary music curriculum was a success as shown by data from HMI and OFSTED inspections. In fact, primary teachers have stolen the honours from secondary music teachers: OFSTED found that the quality of music teaching at Key Stage 2 'typically exceeds that in all other NC subjects' whereas 'in KS3 it is usually lower than that in the remainder of the curriculum' (OFSTED, 1995, p. 3). They found that the quality of pupils' learning in the primary school tailed off at the end of the Key Stage 2 and into Key Stage 3.

It might have been supposed that the high quality of primary music lessons was accounted for by the fact that they were taken by music specialists. However, it turns out (OFSTED, 1995, p. 18) that the responsibility for teaching music was being transferred from the music specialist to the class teacher:

> A large majority of class music lessons are taught by the pupils' own class teacher.

Indeed, in the HMI survey of the first year of the National Curriculum for music, and again in OFSTED inspections 1995–6, it was found that there were no significant differences in the quality of the teaching by specialists and generalist class teachers (Mills, 1997). Further, there was sometimes a problem that music specialists had not extended their work to composition, but continued to offer a curriculum which was derived from their own musical skills and knowledge:

> many music specialists have not revised the curriculum they offer in Y1 to Y4 to reflect the Programmes of Study, and over-emphasize the use of staff notation, which is not required in KS2, or singing at the expense of composing and appraising.
>
> (OFSTED, 1995, p. 18)

It would appear, then, that not only are class teachers good music teachers, but also that their specialist colleagues may be the ones who are restricting the development of the music curriculum.

Conclusion

To some it may be surprising that generalist class teachers are doing such good music teaching, given their supposed 'lack of musical skills'. However, as is being argued throughout this book, children's learning will only improve when the music curriculum is handed over to the class teacher, when musical activities are handed over to children and the music curriculum becomes an integral part of the primary curriculum. The quality will be further improved when the class teacher is supported by a skilled music co-ordinator. Chapter 9 will give further guidance on how the class teacher can be supported by the music co-ordinator.

The National Curriculum took primary music beyond singing with piano accompaniment and to a range of musical activities for all children within the scope of the class teacher. To gain statutory approval for this against the political forces of elitism and ignorance was a great success. No longer is music simply an accompaniment to school assemblies and performances, nor will it be for just a selection of 'musical' children. The statutory provision for children gives teachers and schools the opportunity to make a good all-round music curriculum for all children in performing, composing and appraising music. This brings it much closer to the richness of individual learning and expression of individual ideas which is possible in children's language work, reading and writing.

On 1 May 1997 the new Labour Government 'hit the ground running' with hearty ambitions for a whole series of new targets to be achieved. In education one of these was to be the national strategies for the improvement of literacy and numeracy. This was a continuation of the centralizing tendency for the government to dictate not only curriculum content, but also teaching methods and timing. Inevitably this led to a lessening of priorities for the other foundation subjects, including music, with the Secretary of State, David Blunkett, announcing that schools could relax the statutory requirements for them. Sir Simon Rattle again reappeared with a letter in *The Times* (21 January 1998) warning of the threat to music and, thereby, the nation's cultural heritage.

At the time of writing (April 1998) with the new National Curriculum for the year 2000 approaching and the government's grip on the core subjects tightening, the role of music as a statutory subject seems threatened. However, music's ten years as a subject in the National Curriculum has changed its status and content from singing on Friday afternoons to children exploring their own musical experience and knowledge as part of an enlarged primary curriculum.

References

Alexander, R. (1984) *Primary Teaching.* London: Holt, Rinehart and Winston.

Ashton, P. M. E., Kneen, P., Davies, F. and Holley, B. J. (1975) *The Aims of Primary Education: A Study of Teachers' Opinions.* London: Macmillan.

Bennett, N. and Dunne, E. (1992) *Managing Classroom Groups.* Hemel Hempstead: Simon & Schuster.

Blenkin, G. M. and Kelly, A. V. (1981) *The Primary Curriculum.* London: Harper & Row.

Coulby, D. (1996) The construction and implementation of the primary core curriculum. In D. Coulby, S. Ward (eds), *The Primary Core National Curriculum: Policy into Practice* (2nd edition). London: Cassell.

Cox, B. (1991) *Cox on Cox: An English Curriculum for the 1990s*. Sevenoaks: Hodder & Stoughton.

DES (1978) *Primary Education in England*. London: HMSO.

DES (1991a) *Aspects of Primary Education: The Teaching and Learning of Music*. London: HMSO.

DES (1991b) *Music in the Primary Schools of Wales*. HMI Occasional Paper. Cardiff: Welsh Office.

DES (1991c) *Primary Education: A Statement by the Secretary of State for Education and Science Kenneth Clarke*. London: DES.

DES (1991d) *Aspects of Primary Education in France: A Report by HMI*. London: HMSO.

DES (1992) *National Curriculum: Draft Order for Music*. London: DES.

DES and Welsh Office (1988) *English for Ages 5 to 11*. London: DES and Welsh Office.

DES and Welsh Office (1991a) *National Curriculum Music Working Group Interim Report*. London: DES and Welsh Office.

DES and Welsh Office (1991b) *Music for Ages 5 to 14: Proposals of the Secretary of State for Education and Science and the Secretary of State for Wales*. London: DES and Welsh Office.

Edwards, D. and Mercer, N. (1987) *Common Knowledge*. Milton Keynes: Open University Press.

Galton, M., Simon, B. and Croll, P. (1980) *Inside the Primary Classroom*. London: Routledge & Kegan Paul.

Gulbenkian Foundation (1982) *The Arts in Schools*. Borough Green: Novello.

Hoggart, R. (1957) *The Uses of Literacy*. Harmondsworth: Penguin.

Mills, J. (1997) OFSTED Music Inspection Findings 1995–6 *Primary Music Today*, Issue 8.

Mortimore, P., Sammons, P., Stoll, L., Lewis, D. and Ecob, R. (1988) *School Matters: The Junior Years*. London: Open Books.

NCC, (1992) *Music in the National Curriculum: A Report to the Secretary of State for Education and Science on the Statutory Consultation for Attainment Targets and Programmes of Study in Music*. York: National Curriculum Council.

O'Hear, A. (1991) Out of sync with Bach. *Times Educational Supplement*, 22 February.

OFSTED (1995) *Music: A Review of Inspection Findings*. London: HMSO.

Plowden Report (1967) *Children and Their Primary Schools*. Report of the Central Advisory Council for Education in England. HMSO: London.

Pratt, G. and Stephens, J. (1995) *Teaching Music in the National Curriculum*. Oxford: Heinemann.

Rainbow, B. (1984) Introduction to M. A. Langdale and S. Macpherson (eds), *Early Essays on Musical Appreciation (1908–1915)*. Kilkenny, Ireland: Boethius Press.

Ritchie, R. (1996) Science in the National Curriculum. In D. Coulby and S.

Ward (eds), *The Primary Core National Curriculum: Policy into Practice* (2nd edition). London: Cassell.

Robinson, K. (1991) Stop the art breaker. *Times Educational Supplement,* 29 November.

Simon, B. (1981) The primary school revolution: myth or reality? In B. Simon and J. Willcocks (eds), *Research and Practice in the Primary School.* London: Routledge & Kegan Paul.

Smith, F. (1978) *Reading.* Cambridge: CUP.

Swanwick, K. (1992) Facts will put damper on music. *Times Educational Supplement,* 24 January.

Ward, D. (1992) Boulez joins protests against music curriculum. *Guardian,* 17 February.

Ward, S. (1996) Thematic approaches to the core National Curriculum. In D. Coulby and S. Ward *The Primary Core National Curriculum: Policy into Practice* (2nd edition). London: Cassell.

Waterland, L. (1985) *Read with Me: An Apprenticeship Approach to Reading.* London: Thimble Press.

Wood, S. (1991) *Back to Back Memories.* Leeds: Leeds Talking Magazine for the Blind Association.

CHAPTER 3
Performing, Composing, Listening and Appraising
Joanna Glover

Programmes of Study

This chapter introduces the range of activities which have formed the basis of music as it has developed within the National Curriculum, giving an overview of how these can be planned for and assessed. The key to planning for music learning is an understanding of the multiple processes which are involved in composing, performing, listening and appraising and the way these relate to each other in musical activity. The processes are outlined and discussed in relation to children's development of musical skills, knowledge and understanding. Teachers need to be clear about the range of processes in which to involve pupils and about the learning potential in each. This clarifies what to look for in assessing work and gathering evidence on which to base reporting and End of Key Stage Descriptions.

The three main strands of musical activity which are identified in the attainment targets for End of Key Stage Descriptions are *performing, composing,* and *listening and appraising.* It is essential that these be taught in an integrated way so that each contributes to the development of the others. This was the intention of the original Music Working Group (DES and Welsh Office, 1991):

> we believe that the activities of performing, composing and appraising (through active listening) should be interwoven, with the learning derived from each serving to reinforce and develop learning and skill in the others.

As in other National Curriculum subjects it should be remembered that the attainment target structure is a framework for assessment purposes only. For children, particularly younger ones, the relationships between the three activities is extremely fluid. Children's musical activity moves freely between making up their own music and reproducing music they know, so the boundary between composing and performing is indistinct. In many adult musical styles and cultural contexts there is also a complex relationship between performing and composing, where improvising within a set of conventions takes a place somewhere between the two. This may apply to a whole musical system, such as that of North

Indian classical music, in which the skills of a performer encompass improvisation of the music itself according to a complex and intricate traditional practice. It may also apply to parts of systems: for example, a soloist's improvisation within a blues format or an eighteenth-century Western classical concerto. Listening and appraising is an integral and important part of all composing and performing. It may also be approached through movement or as an audience activity. It is central to all work in music and inseparable from other activities. Additionally, performing will often demand an understanding of the historical or cultural aspects of the music; in this case listening to and appraising other music will become part of the preparation for performance.

Planning for music, therefore, needs to take account of the whole range of available relationships and to make it possible for children to move freely between these activities. For this reason Chapters 5 and 6 are organized in accordance with the ways in which practical approaches might be used in the classroom rather than with National Curriculum Attainment Targets. Nevertheless, the attainment target structure must be used alongside the planning of activities as a framework for learning objectives and their assessment within integrated work. This chapter and the next are intended to help lay the groundwork for planning and assessment.

Awareness of musical processes

The attainment target structure helps teachers to focus on what children actually do when they are involved with music. This is important since all too often the attention in music teaching has been almost exclusively on the musical 'object' – the song or the piece – without thought being given to the detail of the processes involved in engaging with music. This is partly related to the familiar issue in teaching of achieving an appropriate balance between process and product and the need for curriculum planning which is based on clear identification of the processes in which the child is to be involved. But it also stems from a misconception about the nature of the musical 'product' itself. As with any time-based art, the essence of music is itself process. Music always has to be made, every time, and it has to be experienced newly every time. In this sense, all music is made only once ever. And the balance between the contribution within music-making of the creative, the interpretative and the interactive is an intricate and almost infinitely variable one. For example:

> In *music made as played*, such as a xylophone piece improvised on
> the spot by two six-year-olds together, the creative (making it up)

and the interactive (exchanging and transforming ideas as the music goes along) are predominant. But there will be an element of interpretation as each child takes up the ideas of the other, understanding them in their own way.

In a *song sung by the class,* learnt from the teacher, there will be an interpretative element (all the musical nuances of how the song is sung: its speed, character, quality of voice) which may be more or less creative according to how far teacher and children have felt able to make the song their own.

From the second example the question arises of who has taken control of the musical processes involved in the re-creation of the song for singing together. On this occasion it may be the teacher who set the speed, gave the song a character, and managed the way it slowed down at the end. If it is always the teacher, however, the children will be excluded from first-hand experience of these interpretative processes and blocked at the point where they put their learning to use and practise it for themselves. They will have missed out a whole dimension of the perform- ing process. This is not uncommonly the case, yet can easily be avoided by keeping a clear view of:

i)   music itself as process;
ii)   the detail of the processes involved in musical activity.

The teacher's role here is to be clear about what processes are involved and to make sure that each child has the opportunity to develop capability, understanding and knowledge within them. There are equal opportunities issues here too. For example, awareness is needed concern- ing gender roles and stereotyping within musical activity. Boys and girls can be encouraged to take both directing and participatory roles, to use the range of instruments, including voices and information technology, with confidence, and to participate in all styles of music. At the same time there should be sensitivity to gender aspects of traditional musics when, for example, in some cultures there might be music which is performed exclusively by women or men. For example, Kwami (1991) shows the importance of age–gender classifications in West African musics and discusses implications of these in selecting music for curricular use. And the musical sensitivities within certain religious faiths should be remem- bered.

The teacher's awareness of the musical processes in which children should be engaged forms the basis of practical provision in units of work. With this in view, the process aspects of the three main activities will be considered in turn, with the cautionary reminder that in practice each will grow out of the other.

Listening and appraising

Listening and appraising are the core skills in all musical activity. They are central to all those occasions on which children listen critically to their own and others' music, as part of performing or composing and as audience listeners. It is crucial to children's musical development that this is recognized and that teaching always focuses on developing sensitive and responsive listening, whatever the activity. Listening and appraising are therefore also the key *teaching* skills for music; all assessment of music making depends on the teacher listening to and appraising children's work. For this reason, despite Listening and Appraising being Attainment Target 2 (England) or 3 (Wales), they are discussed first here. Although there is a group of activities particularly identified in the programmes of study under the heading of Listening and Appraising (DFE, 1995, para 6, England), these cannot be seen in isolation or as being the only ones through which children develop listening and appraising skills. Flynn and Pratt (1995) show how wide ranging the opportunities for developing these skills can be.

Some examples of *listening and appraising* in practice might be:

> An infant class listen together to a piece of electronic music which uses all sorts of different sound events and qualities of sound in lines, swoops and bursts. They talk about what happens in the music with the help of a score which the teacher has built up in front of them using coloured sticky paper. Later they make a movement sequence to go with it.

> Two children listen on headphones in the music area to recording of Elizabethan English dance music in connection with work on Tudor history. They listen to a galliard and a pavane performed by an early music group and report back to the class on the different rhythms, speeds and moods of the dances and the kinds of steps and gestures that the music suggests. They later practise playing another dance tune themselves using recorder and drum; they try to recreate the 'feel' of the music they've heard.

> Four children are composing a group piece based on the ideas of predictability and surprise. They play a draft version of their music through and discuss its surprise element. They are so bound up with playing the music that they find it hard to assess its effectiveness. They record the music and listen to it on tape with

two other children. Discussion with the newcomers helps to suggest ways of making the surprise more dramatic. They resume playing and modify the piece.

The class listen together to some music from the Andes for pan-pipes, guitar and drums. They discuss the way in which the different layers of the music fit together: in the foreground a freely moving tune; behind it a rhythmic, chordal guitar accompaniment, over a simple repetitive drum pattern. An interest in the techniques of layering has arisen from the composing work of two small groups in the class and the music is compared with these children's work.

A child chooses a tape from the class listening library and listens during a quiet reading session in the classroom. She makes an entry in her listening diary, recording her choice and her personal review of the music.

Two classes together learn and practise a new song for assembly. Children take turns at being part of a small listening group who give feedback to the others on how the singing sounds: how clear the words are, how well children keep together, which are the difficult parts of the tune to pitch accurately. The children also work on trying to listen to themselves and other people while they sing. They are asked for suggestions on how to do this.

Listening and appraising form part of all practical music-making as composers or performers try out their work, listen critically to it and modify it in the light of their appraisal. Active listening to music performed live or on tape or disc is an essential part of musical experience and a prime means by which children extend their musical understanding and enrich their fund of imaginative ideas. The listening response – physical, intellectual and emotional – is at the heart of music and should be treated with care. Children should be encouraged to find and focus on this response in themselves and should learn ways of drawing on it within the whole range of musical activity.

It is difficult to treat the processes involved in listening and appraising separately. They are clearly quite different activities, each with their own skills. But since how we hear music is so intrinsically bound up with the kind of appraising attention we bring to it, for teaching purposes it is useful to take the two together.

Developing listening and appraising is dependent on developing a whole climate for music listening throughout the school. High expectations of listening carefully and responding individually to music take time

45

to become a way of life. Gradually these can be established by reinforcing a common approach to the range of musical occasions:

- finding quiet for individual and small group playing or singing;
- using headphones for solo or group listening to recorded music;
- focusing class attention for hearing work presented live or on tape, for discussing music listened to together;
- listening to music through dance;
- listening as a larger audience in assembly or to visiting performers.

The aim is for music to be associated with spaces of quiet or of stimulating, enjoyable sound and not, as is often the case and usually without foundation, with noise, disruption and issues of control. Doing less, with better quality, is always preferable to a room full of cacophony.

An important factor in establishing the common approach throughout the school is the simple strategy of agreeing a common vocabulary in which to talk about music and an understood framework of different types of talk, reflecting different ways in which we describe or articulate responses to music. These can then be built on as children progress through the school, ensuring a continuity of approach. Since this vocabulary will also be the foundation for assessment in music, it is important that children understand it for themselves and are aware of their own developing abilities in listening and appraising as a central core in all their music learning. They will learn to appraise their own performing and composing along the same lines they use when appraising other music they listen to. The following is an outline of the key processes which might form the basis of children's listening and appraising activity.

ACTIVE LISTENING

This begins with skills of concentration and learning to listen intently. Children may need to be shown how to focus their attention on what they are hearing. The teacher can model listening behaviour, showing through body language and responses what it is to listen, follow and respond to music. This means joining in with listening with the children, becoming fully involved in the music and expecting them to do the same. Listening with eyes shut, lying down, sitting in a group, with movement or following a score each offer different kinds of opportunity. Listening activities should be valued in practical ways and time made for a range of opportunities, just as time is made for reading or listening to a story.

For recorded music, children should be able to choose to listen privately to tapes from the class collection with headphones, comfortably in a quiet atmosphere. There should be focused listening activities for individuals or small groups. The class should listen together in contexts ranging from informal listening for musical pleasure to more formal, critical listening and appraisal, and to listening through dance. In all situations the emphasis should be on the quality of experience. Using good-quality equipment, choosing a good time and allowing enough of it, finding a place which is quiet and spacious enough to give both music and listeners room can all contribute significantly to the depth of listening experiences.

AURAL PERCEPTION

Whether the music is live or recorded, the process of following music as it goes along, as it develops and changes, requires considerable concentration. As children's understanding develops, the skills of an increasingly active listening process can develop alongside. Active listening depends on *aural perception*. Children's perception of sound is normally very acute. They will build their perception of musical patterns, structures and qualities through listening experience if it is supported by talk and practical work focusing on aspects of the musical elements. For example, a focus on melodic movement might look at how a melody sounds when it moves by smaller or larger steps or by wide jumps; how it stays still or moves on by using longer or shorter note values; and how the feeling of movement is enhanced by variations in timbre, intensity and dynamics as the line is played or sung. Children's aural perception in music is often blunted by low expectations and lack of subtlety in teaching approaches. If they are only expected to distinguish loud from quiet or 'going up' from 'coming down', they quickly stop using the full range of their aural sensitivity at the very age when it is at its height. Young children readily grasp musical subtleties if attention is drawn to them. The difficulty is, however, that in music context is everything. Any musical idea extracted in order to be discussed must immediately be returned to the whole musical context in which it has its meaning. So discussions, as above, of a melodic example should be followed by just hearing, playing or singing the full piece again in order to listen and respond to the effect of the whole.

Listening to music involves not just the ears but the whole body as a sensor. This applies to all of us and we could all learn to be more aware of the way our whole bodies pick up sound. Sounds of different timbre, pitch and dynamic are felt quite differently. Compare, for example, listening to a large deep wooden chime bar with listening to a small

47

woodblock. An average class is likely to contain at least one or two children who have some temporary hearing loss or more permanent hearing disability. This is not a problem. Listening in a musical context can be of positive benefit to all such children. Consideration can be given to where a child is sitting in relation to the sound source, particularly in a live music context and particular attention given to the widest range of opportunities for sensing music through the body, for example, physical contact with the vibrating surface, feeling sound through the floor. Care should be taken with children who use hearing aid devices which may need to be adjusted or removed for music listening.

DESCRIBING AND ANALYSING THE MUSIC

Children will talk readily about music in all sorts of ways. One of the teacher's roles is to help them sort out and use different kinds of talk within the musical context. There can be a tendency for discussion with children to go straight to questions of taste: 'Did you like it?' or even outside music altogether: 'What did it remind you of?' These are both valid questions in some situations, but they cannot be used to replace talk about the music itself. So it is helpful to think about the different processes that talk is engaging the children in. The most important of these from the point of view of developing children's grasp of the music they are hearing is the process of describing and analysing the music itself. This might be children's music – their own or others' – or recorded music being introduced as listening or performing repertoire. Children can listen and be asked to say what they heard, to describe the music. They will do this with whatever language they have and the musical vocabulary they use can gradually be extended as it becomes clear that the children have a grasp of what it applies to. The teacher may need to model this kind of talk, introducing new vocabulary and picking out points to listen for. Having simply described the music in terms of its elements, of rhythm, melody, dynamics, form, timbre (see Chapter 5, page 74ff.), discussion can go on to analysis of the way it has been constructed. There may be one or two musical patterns which have been used all through in different ways, or ideas that gradually alter and grow. Recognizing these is the first stage of appraising. It is fundamental to performing music sensitively, to understanding composing techniques, and to gaining insight into any music which is being listened to.

INVESTIGATING CONTEXT

Making sense of why music is as it is involves children investigating and developing an understanding of the context in which a particular piece has been made. If they are listening to music of other times and places, this will include its historical and cultural context, the social situation of the women or men who make or made it, and the kind of occasion for which it has been used or composed. Research will be needed to find out the facts as far as they are available but contextualizing should be seen as a process which also involves questioning, imagination, empathizing and thought. If it is to play a lively part in children's appraisal of music and in their own performing it needs to go well beyond collecting information. Children can use a range of sources – poems, pictures, interviews, etc. – which together with straightforward reference material can prompt a breadth of thinking and a deeper understanding. They can then be helped to apply these to the music itself, to how it is made, played and heard, and to how it is responded to.

EVALUATING THE MUSIC

There will be times when it is appropriate for children to evaluate music they have heard or made. This is a matter of making judgements about the music that are informed and reach beyond personal taste. Children should learn to think about criteria for evaluating music, taking into account its context and purpose. Any music must be evaluated in its own terms, and children can discuss which aspects of it, such as technical skills or dramatic effect, are to be considered relevant. Evaluating involves articulating reasons for the judgements made. Children can be encouraged to support their judgements with thoughtful reasoning, going beyond 'I like/don't like it'. When evaluating music composed or performed by others in the class, the teacher can help children to evaluate the music in a way that respects and values the work of those who made it. Such evaluation should be allowed to emerge as a concern only when children have had considerable experience of making and listening to their own music.

RESPONDING

Underlying all aspects of musical activity is responding to the music itself. Children readily respond to music in a variety of ways and this can be encouraged and built on. At different times children may simply listen, responding inwardly and no more, or they may respond in discussion, in movement, through writing descriptively or creatively, or through painting or other art media. And, if the prevailing approach is right, their music-making will be full of the life and feeling which are at the heart of musical sensitivity. The teacher's role in fostering this is crucial, and much depends on the expectations and treatment of children's responses. An understanding can be established that different people respond to different music in different ways and that each person's reactions and tastes are to be respected. A climate can be created which supports genuine involvement and a creativity of response which draws on both intellect and emotion.

Performing

Within AT1 *performing* covers all music-making with voices and with instruments where pupils are performing their own or others' compositions within class and for a variety of wider audiences. It includes all the skills of controlling the sound produced and shaping the music with understanding and the skills of participating in group music-making, either directing or being directed. It also includes use of visual signs and some form of notation in a performance context.

Some examples of *performing* in practice might be:

> working out and repeatedly playing a known tune by ear on an instrument;

> learning a song with the class, then practising it in pairs, using words and perhaps a reminder notation on card; later, singing and teaching it to a small group of younger children;

> preparing songs and incidental music for a class drama to be performed for parents;

> as a group of three, practising music composed last week for performance to the rest of the class.

Choice of music for performing should reflect a multicultural approach in all ways. Music should be drawn from a range of times, places and cultures while styles and contexts should be understood. The following is an outline of the processes which might form the basis of children's performing experience under AT1. These are introduced under headings which, though they relate loosely as a sequence, are for convenience only and do not represent a pattern to be followed.

EXPLORING INSTRUMENTS AND THE VOICE

There is a whole range of perceptual and physical skills to be built up through exploring the voice and other instruments in both teacher-led and free 'play' or self-directed situations. Learning to take sound seriously – to control all aspects of it in order to obtain the musical effect wanted – is a matter of continuing exploration and practice. It involves establishing cause and effect in the production of sound by listening and doing together, and by learning to judge the outcome aesthetically. Such exploration continues to be important at every level of performing capability. Children should be able to work with a range of instruments, both pitched and unpitched, and need time to concentrate on the potential of each particular instrument, including the voice, in both exploratory and musical contexts. They need to listen carefully as they sing or play, and they need feedback on how it sounds. Playing techniques and instruments can be modified for children with disabilities; instruments can be mounted on stands and clamped into accessible positions, or devices constructed to enable the child to control, for example, a beating or plucking action.

LEARNING THE MUSIC

This involves being able to bring to life by singing or playing what we might call the musical 'text' itself. This text is not necessarily written down, though it may be. It is the piece of music to be performed as far as it is given by the composer or handed on by another performer – the tune, the drum pattern, the parts made to fit together or whatever it may be. Differentiating in order to match each child's vocal or instrumental capabilities is important here so that there is a balance between the challenge of gaining new technical skills and having enough fluency to make music in *a musical way*.

LEARNING THE PROCEDURES OF THE MUSIC

With some music, it is more appropriate to talk about learning its procedures. Where the music is to be entirely or partly improvised, the processes here will be those of becoming familiar with the framework to be used. This may be an outline plan: for example, 'the music will have everyone joining in one at a time and then dropping out in reverse order' or a more specific musical structure such as a chord progression over which players will improvise in turn.

INTERPRETING

Learning the music is inseparable from interpreting it and this involves deciding how to sing or play the given material. This is a matter of being aware of, and *controlling*, all the variables, such as timing, speed, dynamics and timbre, and of *shaping* the music with sensitivity. The procedure here is to 'Listen and Decide' (Loane, 1988), to try out many ways and choose the most satisfactory for the time being. There is rarely a single right way to interpret a piece, though there may be ways that are inappropriate or which do not work. This is the creative process through which the performer responds to what is given and makes it his or her own. Children are able to do this with empathy and imagination from an early age and the old instrumental teaching approach of 'we'll learn the notes first and then put in the expression' misses altogether the intimacy of the connection between what 'the notes' are and how they are played.

Some of a performer's interpretation of a piece is worked out or pre-rehearsed, but part of it happens on the wing, and it is important to allow for practising both of these creative responses. The children themselves must always be involved in the processes of interpretation. The teacher can help by focusing attention on the choices to be made, or by encouraging children to listen to and compare different interpretations of a single piece. The teacher should not 'do' the interpretation for the child, nor, for instance, give the impression that notated instructions such as 'forte' (loud, strong) written under a passage can be 'obeyed' in a mechanistic way without judgement.

A further dimension of interpretation is that of researching the background to the particular type of music in question, the conventions of its performance as connected with its cultural roots in time or place, and making decisions as to how far these will influence the performance of a piece. Different interpretations of medieval or classical music, deriving from scholarly research, model how children can be encouraged to approach performance. A reception class who have enthusiastically lived with and compared in detail three versions of Mozart's 'Turkish' Rondo have begun to absorb for themselves the subtleties of the idea of 'same but different' which underlies the making of music at simple or complex levels.

The National Curriculum Music documents were surprisingly silent on the interpretative aspects of music. These aspects of music-making relate to issues both of quality (making music musically) and of control (who makes the musical decisions). In the interests of real music learning it is crucial that they are valued and form a central part of every pupil's performing experience.

PLAYING OR SINGING A WHOLE PIECE ALL THROUGH WITHOUT STOPPING

This is something like taking flight, travelling, coming in for a landing, and touching down. From the participant's point of view, whether the music is improvised or composed, just keeping going in itself needs managing physically and mentally. Some of the interpretative shaping processes can only be experienced when music is performed 'whole'. At a more basic level, simply finding a fluency or a right pace and maintaining these may be a challenge. This is also the point at which the full impact of the experience of music begins to be felt and the performer's sense of this feeds back into the musical interpretation so that the music becomes *drama.*

PRESENTING MUSIC

There are different levels of performing music. Presenting music to other listeners entails processes concerned with the element of *communicating* the musical performance to those who are 'out there', not participating. Children need time to think about what is involved in this. They can consider ways of *projecting* the music and also be encouraged to be aware of the listeners and to respond to them. This interaction with an audience is another element which feeds back into the music itself and becomes part of the excitement of live performance in which performers and listeners collaborate. This is learnt through children being shown how to be both supportive, active listeners and communicative performers.

When children present their work to others in the class it should be agreed by all what kind of an occasion this is. For individual and small group work it is useful to have 'sharing' sessions where work in progress or almost completed is brought to the larger group for discussion rather than applause. Presenting work to the class as an audience then becomes a further stage which deserves attention in its own right.

PERFORMING FOR AN AUDIENCE

More formal performance situations introduce a further set of processes. Here children rehearse towards an occasion. The additional aspect of 'getting it right on the night' brings the need for choosing an appropriate programme, having enough practice to achieve security with the musical material, preparing for a particular audience and location and polishing details of presentation such as starts and finishes. There is a higher 'adrenalin factor' to handle and children need to experience and then learn to manage this, as well as the practicalities of where to position themselves to perform, and how to respond to applause.

PERFORMING FOR TAPE-RECORDING

This introduces yet more considerations. Children can learn to consider what will be a suitable sound environment for a tape recording, how to limit unwanted noise, where to situate the microphone and to test and monitor recording levels. If a multi-track unit is available, more sophisticated processes of 'miking up', balancing and mixing come into play. It is important to treat recording, even at the simplest level, as part of an aesthetic process and to aim for the best possible quality.

PRACTISING

All the above involve practice. Although practising has always been expected in association with learning an instrument, classroom music has often allowed little or no opportunity for children to practise their work. In a time-based art, practice is essential for work of quality and children should be helped to do this productively, whatever kind of instrument they are using, including voice. They are often very well motivated to find times for individual work and to try ideas and techniques over and over again until they have accomplished them. The teacher can capitalize on this natural process of self-challenge and children should not have to plead to be allowed to stay in at break to practise when this is intrinsic to the demands of the music curriculum. The manual dexterity required for some instruments needs frequent exercise for the player just to keep physically 'in training'. Repetition need not be mindless but allows for developing control of timbre, timing and dynamic nuance as well as trying out different ways with the music.

READING FROM NOTATION

Reading is important as a means of accessing music for performance, mainly through the 'staff notation' traditionally used in Western music. The ability to do this can be built up gradually from the early years but must follow becoming familiar with the musical sounds themselves and never be taught in isolation from them. Several approaches to notation can be combined (see Chapters 5 and 6), but in connection with performance the following may be borne in mind. Throughout the primary school, most children's ability to perform will outstrip their ability to read notation for live performance. Their performance work must not be limited to what they can read, either for voice or for instruments. They should have access to notations of the music they learn and at times follow it whilst performing or listening to recordings of performances, even if they are unable to read from it fully. They should be introduced gradually both to the detail of 'decoding' signs for particular pitches, rhythm values and more holistically to the use of space on a page in relation to time and pitch, texture and harmony, so that the process of learning is both one of building up a vocabulary and of becoming familiar with the system generally. They should understand the relation of score to music and its limitations: what it cannot tell the player. This is crucial since often it is the approach to reading music which dulls the child's sensitivity as a performer to those elements which cannot be recorded on the page, for example, rhythmic and melodic nuance, timbre and dynamics.

Composing

Within AT1 *composing* covers all activities involving 'making up' music. This includes improvising, in which the music is made up as the singer or player goes along. Some examples of *composing* in practice might be:

> A child offers to sing a song to the class. The song is made up on the spot; it tells a made-up story and uses a verse pattern similar to many the class have sung before.

> Three children decide to make a piece for drums involving having 'conversations' with each other. To begin with they improvise as a group, listening to each other and copying and transforming each other's ideas; later they 'fix' a version of the music.

> Two children spend most of an afternoon working out music for two xylophones. They agree on a simple tune which they play together and then work out two ways of varying it, by changing the rhythm and by playing it as a round. They put all this together and play it with great attention to detail: of dynamics, of which beaters are used, and of fitting together as planned. The music is recorded on tape.

> Some music is needed for a bridge-building scene in a class drama; the class decide that the music should use wood on wood and metal on metal sounds only and that for its musical structure it should have a slow beat with rhythm patterns layered over it. These ideas are all suggested by the movements of the actors. A group of five children is commissioned to make the piece.

As will be seen in later chapters the process of composing can take many different forms. These are influenced by the practical opportunities or constraints of the working situation and the ways of working which suit individual children. The following is an outline of some of the processes which might form part of children's experience in composing.

PLAYING WITH MUSIC

Young children need the opportunity to play musically just as they need to play with water or sand in order to build their basic experience of the materials, what Crowe (1983) terms 'the feel of things'. Musical play is about the 'materials' of music – sounds and their patterns – and also musical behaviour and interaction with others: a silly sing-song conversation, for example. Music comes naturally into children's play and this is a source of creativity which flows into composing activity of a more organised kind. Continuing to engage in musical play activity can contribute vitality to the music of any composer, however experienced s/he may be.

EXPLORING THE MEDIUM

Arising from play, the exploration of sounds and their behaviour alone and together, of sound 'gestures', patterns of sounds, sound and silence (doing and not doing), is a prerequisite of all music-making. Children composing need the opportunity to discover how individual instruments, including the voice, work. Any composer must understand how sounds are made and controlled, what the available ranges of timbres, pitch, dynamics and so on are for the particular instrument for which music is to be composed. The medium for composition may also be electronic; children can explore a range of music technology.

They also need sustained opportunities to explore ways of building sounds into musical ideas and structures, rather than stopping short at sound-making. For both play and exploration a music area is needed, for access by individual children, equipped with a range of sound sources and ideas cards, and given regular focus by class discussion and pooling of 'finds'. This should be quiet enough for children to hear what they are doing and should be a stimulating and constantly evolving provision. Exploration is a serious business. The spirit of exploration at best combines the driving sense of excitement at the possibilities opening up ahead with the discipline of thorough investigation and observation of detail. The teacher's role must be to encourage both of these in the children's attitude to the exploration of sound and of musical ideas.

IMPROVISING ALONE OR IN A GROUP

Improvising involves working creatively with musical ideas as they arise from singing or playing and interactively as they are exchanged with other performers. It is an important form of music-making in its own right, combining aspects of both performance and composition. Many musics have an element of improvisation in them, such as a classical concerto with a solo cadenza. Some are almost entirely improvisatory, with performers improvising on given material as in some jazz traditions.

Improvising can also be a dynamic force in the composing process, a way of getting ideas flowing and working out material. Addison (1988) discusses these and further distinctions between improvisatory approaches and links improvisation to play activity. Children should have the opportunity to improvise in a variety of ways. They may work alone, using exploration of an instrument itself as a framework or as a pair, deciding on an outline structure such as a conversation between two instruments, as a group trying a 'joining in one at a time' piece or an improvisation over a repeating melodic pattern. Improvisation contributes significantly to the development of listening skills, by demanding of a player immediate response to what is happening musically.

The three processes of *play*, *exploration* and *improvisation* are fundamental to composing in that each, in a particular and practical way, draws creatively on musical resources within and allows for these to emerge in such a way as to feed into the compositional process. They allow room for trying out and assimilating musical ideas which have been observed and borrowed as well as those which arise newly from the players, instruments or materials themselves. Time allowed for children to immerse themselves with concentration in these activities will be well spent. If children are expected to compose without such opportunities, the results will be of very poor quality, since they will largely be 'guesses' governed more by luck than by experience and judgement. This is why flexible timetabling is essential to high-quality composition work.

There is no single sequence of processes that can be said to characterize the work of all composers. One of the interesting aspects of working with children composing is the variety of ways in which they arrive at and then deal with their musical ideas (see Chapter 7). The following may give the teacher some indication of how children might move from any of the three preliminary processes above towards shaping a finished composition; however, these should not be regarded as fixed procedures. Throughout children should have the opportunity to work both alone and with others, devising their own musical purposes and working on tasks that focus on specific musical ideas and techniques. The teacher can help children to become aware of the processes (Glover, 1995) and to take control of decision-making.

MOVING FROM IDEA TO FORM

Here a musical idea such as a rhythm pattern, a fragment of melody or a sequence of instrumental sounds is worked gradually into an overall musical shape that becomes the form of the final piece. Having arrived at a stock of ideas through preliminary processes as above, the children will begin *selecting* and *sequencing* some of the material. To do this they should be encouraged to try things through repeatedly, *listening* and *deciding* (on the basis of listening) which ideas they want and in what order. The extent to which they will be able to work with the notions of time sequence and musical events within a temporal structure will obviously depend on the age of the children.

Having got some musical ideas provisionally arranged the child may want to spend some time *developing* these: allowing them to grow or change gradually, to be played by different instruments or with varying dynamic qualities, to be set in contrast or combination with each other or to be highlighted by silence, by a counter idea or used as foreground against an accompaniment.

After further cycles of listening, selecting, sequencing and getting rid of bits that don't work, a *draft* of the composition will be arrived at. The piece can be tried through and its overall shape *reviewed* in terms of how it works, how the material joins up, what the effect on the listener is, how aesthetically satisfactory the structure and so on. These are questions which have both objective and subjective aspects to them. The children must decide but the teacher has an important role in focusing their attention and encouraging judgements that are both thoughtful and musically responsive. There may be several draft and review cycles. Once a final version is fixed, the music can be *saved* (i) in memory, (ii) on tape or (iii) in notation, and consideration can be given to details of performance.

MOVING FROM FORM TO IDEA

Here it is the musical framework that is the starting-point. For example, the music is to be a dialogue between two opposed elements (instruments or motifs) which gradually come to agree, or a song with verses and chorus, or an adding structure which is built up in stages and then reversed. There is an outline sequence already in place. Children need opportunities to evolve these musical purposes and frameworks for themselves. In this case *planning* the rough detail of some of the features of the framework may precede exploring ideas which might fit the bill. The children will know what they are looking for in the way of musical detail and the *listen* and *decide* process will be focused on *selecting and refining* musical ideas according to their role in the framework. The later stages of work, once a draft has been arrived at, may be the same as in the former approach.

This and the previous way of working are based on construction or assembly models of composing, where the final piece is worked out and built up with an awareness of the contributory parts. There are other ways of working which are more holistic.

58

MAKING MUSIC AS A WHOLE

A cautionary note is needed here over some pieces children make which arrive complete, with little or no need or possibility of further work or change. It is a feature of children's work that sometimes their compositions are created by being played or sung straight through and remembered there and then. This is an equivalent perhaps to a through-written poem which is dashed down onto paper without hesitation. Sometimes minor modifications are made; sometimes the child simply sees the piece as a whole which could not be otherwise. These pieces can be highly successful ones and the teacher must in any case accept their instantly fixed nature and not ask the child to 'improve' the work. This would be to misunderstand the whole logic of the situation since, if improved on, it won't be this piece any more. It is wise to go straight to 'save' and then on to the next piece in the series.

BRINGING MUSIC GRADUALLY INTO FOCUS

This strategy is usually associated with improvisation where both shape and ideas begin to emerge as repeatable each time 'through'. By repeated playing, with discussion in between, the music assumes each time more clear-cut features until a final shape becomes apparent with all its detail. The process is one of progressive focusing, with repeated cycles of *do as a whole-review*. Another analogy here might be to a piece of sculpture, with irrelevant material gradually being removed at each stage to reveal the finished object.

Children should be encouraged to engage in the range of these strategies as appropriate and over time. Composition is essentially an individual process; particularly for younger children, most pieces of work will be best done alone or at most with one other child. In collaborations at any age, it will often work best if one person takes the main composing decisions and the result is considered to be his/her piece, albeit using ideas from others if they seem to work. The composition work of each child must always be seen as a series of pieces and not just one-off events, just as the writing should be seen as part of a developing folio. The different ways of working offer different insights into how music works and allow different musical possibilities to emerge. As they gain experience children find processes that particularly suit them as individuals; the teacher should initially at least keep the options open.

The teacher can also help each child to develop a sense of self as a composer, at however simple a level. This emerges partly from reviewing work over time with the child so that a pattern of development is seen. It also comes from seeing classroom work as taking place alongside the work of adult composers. The composer as someone with a creative development of his/her own, making choices and pursuing interests, can become a figure to relate to if discussions on other people's music include information and speculation or empathizing on these aspects. Children should encounter music by women composers (Cant, 1990) and meet live composers of both sexes. Teachers can model composing processes with the children to reinforce understanding, in the way that they do with writing.

Metacognition of Musical Process

If children are to become independent as listeners and appraisers, performers and composers, they need to understand what is involved in these roles and to recognize the processes that contribute to each. This has implications for how the music curriculum is planned. As well as just 'doing' these activities, children can be encouraged to reflect on the processes and understand how to take themselves through them. For example, children can evaluate the effectiveness of different ways of practising a difficult part of a piece for performance, later questioning which might be most useful in subsequent particular contexts; they can discuss the kinds of decisions that must be made by a singer or player interpreting a piece and take turns at making these for the class or group; they can assess their strengths in communicating to an audience, using a list of criteria they have devised themselves beforehand. In composition there are parallels with children gaining an understanding of different writing processes and learning to apply, for example, editing processes for themselves.

Planning can build in opportunities for discussion and reflection on the processes engaged in. Assessment carried out by the teacher with the children can focus on one particular aspect, for example, being able to keep concentration on listening to the music, being able to talk about the music in different ways. Children will gradually gain a *metacognitive* understanding of musical processes, that is, they will experience a process and also be able to reflect on it afterwards and use it for themselves.

References

Addison, R. (1988) A new look at musical improvisation in education. *British Journal of Music Education*, **5**(3), 255–67.

Cant, S. (1990) Women composers and the music curriculum. *British Journal of Music Education*, **7**(1), 5–13.

Crowe, B. (1983) *Play Is a Feeling.* London: Unwin.

DES and Welsh Office (1991) *Music for Ages 5 to 14: Proposals of the Secretary of State for Education and Science and the Secretary of State for Wales.* London: DES and Welsh Office.

DFE (1995) *Music in the National Curriculum.* London: HMSO.

Flynn, P. and Pratt, G. (1995) Developing an understanding of appraising music with practising primary teachers. *British Journal of Music Education* **12**(2), 127–58.

Glover, J. (1995) Listen! – Working with children composing. *Primary Music Today,* Issue 2.

Kwami, R. (1991) An approach to the use of West African musics in the classroom based on age and gender classifications. *British Journal of Music Education,* **8**(2) 119–37.

Loane, B. (1988) *Rudiments of Music* (unpublished).

CHAPTER 4
Assessing, Recording and Reporting Children's Learning in Music
Joanna Glover and Stephen Ward

This chapter is about assessing children's learning in music as a central part of the teaching process. Assessment is taken to include all those occasions on which the teacher observes children working, discusses with a child work on a particular task, and listens to children's work on tape, drawing conclusions about the learning that is taking place.

Assessing children's learning is the key to making sure that children move on and develop musically. It plays an important part in aiding *progression* because it provides the teacher with understanding and information as a basis for *matching* activity or instruction to the child's needs. It is a major factor in sustaining *continuity* at points of transfer from class to class or school to school. In these ways all assessment is *formative* whether it takes place as a small part of an ordinary music session or involves a series of sampling leading to the compiling of a music profile or an End of Key Stage Statement.

Chapters 5 and 6 outline the kinds of musical experiences that are *likely* to be appropriate for children as they move through Key Stages 1 and 2 of the National Curriculum in Music. The theme of this chapter is that the effectiveness of the teacher's provision for these experiences depends on the effectiveness of the ongoing assessment of children's music learning. The processes of assessing are therefore not optional or occasional additions to music teaching, but are intrinsic to it.

Because the two aspects of *assessing* and *ensuring progression* are so closely related, they are considered here together. The discussion covers some aspects of how children learn in music, what kinds of development and progression can be looked for and what strategies can be used in assessing these.

Assessing music demands attention to *each* child's progress. If we are serious about children's learning in music there is no alternative to a teaching approach which has *individual assessment* at its core. This happens in other subjects and it should happen in music.

At the same time we have to be realistic about the pressures and demands of managing a class of primary children and covering the whole curriculum. A sensible level has to be found for assessing learning in a manageable way. In practice, finding such a level and being clear and well organized about what is going to be attempted becomes a contributory factor in reducing pressures. Becoming good at assessing learning in music saves time and energy. Children's motivation and confidence in music is immediately improved once they realize that their work is given serious attention and is expected to develop. This is often the first thing commented on by teachers who begin to work in music in this way; they are astonished at the enthusiasm and learning capacity which is released by this single difference in approach. Further, in assessing music learning the teacher is always assessing other aspects of the curriculum too. Once music is working effectively in a classroom it genuinely enhances much other learning and offers a considerable degree of insight into a child's whole development.

Effective assessment is mainly dependent on a *habitual way of teaching*. It should not imply a great deal of additional time being set aside except at those points where record-keeping and recording are appropriate. These should be brief and limited to what is relevant. If assessing has been fully a part of the normal teaching approach they will draw on information already available.

From the practical point of view, the processes of assessment can be considered in three broad stages:

looking at learning: using a range of teaching skills and strategies to get access to a child's current musical capabilities and understanding;

drawing conclusions about learning: reflecting on what has been observed, leading to conclusions of both the immediate and the more general, longer-term kind; involving the learner in this process;

making use of conclusions: allowing the information and understanding gained by both teacher and child (i) to 'feed forward' into future work and (ii) to be included in a profile or summarized for reporting; letting this contribute towards continuity and accountability.

Each of these is carried out against the background of the teacher's knowledge and experience of how children learn and develop in music, which can only be built up gradually by engaging in the processes of assessment itself and relating what is observed to the findings of others.

When assessment really is made central to the teaching process, the full implications for curriculum planning must be understood and the approach seen as relating to a whole model of learning in music. It will be argued that planning for progression in music cannot take the form of simplistic schemes of what is to be covered during each week or term of the year, where these are determined by a teacher or a published scheme, without reference to assessment of individual children working in a musical context (see also Chapter 9). Planning must be based on an understanding of the children's learning which comes from assessing it. For while the teacher has a music 'agenda' in mind and a repertoire of suitable activities and materials, the weekly and half-termly plans for music will always be evolved:

- to match immediate developments but within a longer-term picture;
- through a process in which teacher and child participate jointly.

Both requirements rely on effective assessment and are essential if teachers are to sustain an approach which challenges children. Assessment cannot be a matter just of simple tests of the 'what do you hear?' type, which give only very limited information, often out of context. The important thing is that children should be working in an atmosphere of high individual expectation which energizes their music. As learners they should take on a sense of themselves as musically capable. This supplies the motivation to practise and acquire relevant skills and the confidence to make music for themselves, to use it as a creative medium. The preconceptions, often strongly modelled by teachers, that some are musical and some are not and that numbers of children are musically 'irretrievable', must be left far behind. As long as, on the basis of assessment, planning allows for children to keep moving on in the ways most appropriate to them and remain confident in their use of the medium, high expectations lead to high achievement for all children.

Learning in music

There is no simple way in which to characterize learning in music. This need not discourage teachers, as the following discussion will show, but it must be recognized and faced up to. The musical development and learning of the child during the primary years are complex and multi-dimensional.

In Chapter 1 it was argued that music is a fundamental form of human *behaviour* and one that develops as a *social practice*, gaining both its specific structures and its significance only within the whole context of living, doing and experiencing. Learning music is therefore dependent both on developmental factors as the child matures, gaining experience and skills, and on a gradual process of initiation into the particular cultural worlds in which the child is growing up. More than this though, music cannot be viewed as an 'add-on' accomplishment or something which simply by craft we learn to construct. A parallel with language may be helpful here.

It has long been recognized that children learn to speak and comprehend oral language within the social context of the family. Children's language develops in an apparently 'natural' way without any direct instruction. Children use grammatical constructions which are peculiar to their stage of development. For example, at two years, the child will say 'daddy home', meaning 'daddy is coming home', and any attempt by the adult to get the child to 'repeat after me ...' in order to rectify and extend the sentence into the adult model is futile. For this reason, the process is known as children's language *acquisition*: that is, children start out with an inherent propensity to be language *users*. Acquisition of the adult system of language rules and vocabulary unfolds gradually in the social context. Having become an effective language-user the child gradually comes to understand language and to be aware of the system: the nature of words, the syntactic structures. It is around the age of four or five that *metalinguistic awareness* of language develops with the onset of literacy and there is a need for knowledge of linguistic terminology: words, letters, sounds, sentences. A sign of such an understanding of language is when children (tiresomely!) become fascinated by jokes which depend on a realization that words have meanings: 'Why can't a car play football? Because it's only got one boot!' In this way children take control of language and use it to manipulate the world and others in it.

In a similar way, from birth the child possesses the propensity for musical action and response which quickly becomes a spontaneous part of play and life generally. Indeed, children's earliest language utterances are often of a musical – that is, musically pitched – kind. Learning in music is learning to *exercise* this behaviour within a whole cultural form of understanding and interaction. Musical understanding is the exercise of a power: it involves 'using' and not just 'having' musical thinking, skills and responses. Coming to understand music is first 'learning to use' – put into action – musical thinking, skills and responses within an already established practice. It is also learning to generate and explore musical purposes: to take musical control. The learner is initiated into what it is to be a 'music-user'.

A wide spectrum of activity is involved here: improvising alone or in a group, composing for self or others, playing or singing music in innumerable different styles, moving to music or just listening to it. And within this spectrum there is a complex network of perceptual skills, physical

skills and interactive skills which contribute in a range of ways; for
example, to singing a song with someone else, or to making an improvised percussion sequence for someone to dance to.

Progression in music learning means building up the following:

> *richness and breadth of music experienced*: of different types and styles
> of music from a range of cultures and contexts, music with
> different moods and character, instrumentation, musical structures
> and techniques;

> *range of experience of different participating and responding roles*:
> singing/playing, without audience and for different audiences;
> moving; listening to music; appraising own and others' music, live
> or recorded; being part of a group improvising or composing; solo
> composing for self or others; collecting music; encountering music
> within different contexts, occasions;

> *skills and applying them* within whole musical contexts: perceptual
> skills, performance skills, interactive skills;

> building *musical thinking* and applying it for own musical purposes:
> developing musical concepts, thinking *in* music, appraising music;

> building a *sense of musical self* through being involved with music:
> own musical history, learning to evolve own musical purposes,
> values preferences, style.

Learning in music cannot therefore be seen as moving along a single
pathway from stage to stage and neither can it be assessed according to
any simple set of criteria which mark the way. There are areas of skill and
knowledge which perhaps might be isolated, targeted and tested against
increasing levels of 'difficulty'. Examples of these might be:

- remembering and reproducing a rhythm heard only once;
- the playing of scales on an instrument;
- the aural analysis involved in recognizing the melodic interval
  between two notes.

The acquisition of abilities of this kind plays a part in learning in music.
However, they are important only in so far as the learner is able to *use*
them within a musical context and are therefore better assessed only
within such a context; different children will require different sets of
abilities at different times; it is impossible to identify a sequence of
developmental priority *between* such sets of abilities. So while curriculum
planning should *allow* for the development of these skills, they cannot be

used to supply the curriculum framework. Learning in music cannot be reduced to set sequences of skill or concept acquisition.

All this should not, however, be taken to imply that planning and assessment for music pose insurmountable problems. Complexity and lack of simple sequence are not obstacles to ensuring that the child progresses nor to efficient assessment; rather they demand that we approach these in particular ways. It may be useful at this point to return to the analogy with language learning. Like music, this involves both individual development and initiation into a shared practice. For example, the following three points made in a report on the findings of the National Writing Project have direct parallels in music:

> An overriding conclusion reached by all project teachers is that writing is a highly complex social practice which cannot be reduced to any simple list of terms or criteria. There is no one type of writing that can represent a writer's ability, nor is it possible to reduce writing ability to a set of isolated components. Neither a monolithic nor a reductive model of language learning is acceptable . . .
>
> We have found no evidence of a linear progression of skills (except in certain one-off achievements in the early years such as alphabetic knowledge) . . .
>
> Writing development is too complex to be reduced to milestones or benchmarks showing 'where one is'. We suggest that a writer's development can be demonstrated best by examples from a number of different tasks supported by commentary which makes clear the context in which they were produced and the criteria by which they were judged.
>
> (Czerniewska, 1988)

These conclusions were reached through the pooling of observations and evidence of how children engage in writing collected by teachers working in their own classrooms. The English National Curriculum statutory orders show the influence of the Project's recognition of these and other features of children's writing development and the models of teaching and assessment implicit in the document embody such an approach, which has been extensively and successfully implemented in classrooms. Once teachers become experienced in knowing what to expect, ways can be found of catering for children's developmental patterns in music, however complex, in the way that they are allowed for in language. In fact, the parallels with language are also of practical help since this is an area in which by and large primary teachers feel more confident.

In music, then, teachers should assess children's development across a range of activities and contexts in which children are operating musically for themselves, and not just under someone else's direction, and using their skills and knowledge towards appropriate musical ends.

Processes of assessment in music

Teachers need to gather evidence on which to base planning which matches children's development, for reporting to parents and for making End of Key Stage Descriptions. This requires a range of strategies which should be planned into ordinary teaching as far as possible. In planning any unit of work it should be clear what assessment strategies are to be used and what range of criteria will be applied. As far as possible these should be made explicit to the children too.

TEACHER OBSERVATION OF CHILDREN WORKING

Observing children working in music is of central importance as a means of access to their learning. Observation will be based on

- *listening* to children's music and their talk about music;
- *watching* children's behaviour as they make and listen to music.

Observation will take place as part of normal teaching with a group, class or individual, but the teacher may need some systematic way of making sure over a period of time that all children are observed. Observing children working on their own is also important, even it if can only be managed for short stretches. This may need some planning, particularly if children usually work somewhere quiet outside the classroom area. Making audio or video tape-recordings can offer further opportunities for listening and looking closely. These can be saved, together with notations or writing, as *evidence* in building a picture of progress.

The teacher can also exploit a range of roles as *participant observer* in relation to the children's activity. These might include taking part in an improvisation with the child, being shown how to sing or play a composition, or having a conversation about music made and heard. *Interacting musically* with children gives a particular kind of insight into their musical understanding which cannot be had by observing from the 'outside'.

Sampling work across the activities of *Performing, Composing, Listening and Appraising* is necessary in obtaining a balanced view since some children respond very differently to the various musical roles. Within these activities, the processes set out in Chapter 3 may be used as a framework against which to look at children's capabilities and learning.

Children should be 'tracked' through a programme of work over time. Most work, particularly in composition, is part of a *series* and one 'look' may be deceptive. The teacher needs to *live with the music* and to recognize how it is bound up in the child's stream of thought and the classroom climate. Given the demands of a normal classroom, thought needs to be given to how to maximize observing opportunities in ways that are realistic. One aspect of this is planning activities which create such opportunities, such as activities which allow the teacher to stand back, or in which the children take turns round a circle.

USING DIAGNOSTIC STRATEGIES

Sometimes it is useful to set up an activity targeting a particular aspect of music learning in order to gain a clearer view of each child's capability. For example, a Year 2 class may make a class tape on which each child is given the chance to sing a song of his or her choice. This can be done in an informal spirit of collaboration as a music and language exercise, with an end product which makes a valuable contribution to the listening library. During preparation it can also give the teacher opportunities to listen carefully to how each child is able to use the singing voice. On a smaller scale, singing games in which children reply to the teacher in turn offer a similar opening and can be very precisely focused to a particular level or skill such as pitching two notes accurately or remembering a pitch shape. In a parallel way, listening to some music and answering specific questions on it can give the teacher some idea of what children are able to describe. When the activity is complete, the teacher reviews the outcomes for each child in relation to the area targeted and uses the information to help with planning future work.

There is a danger with all targeted strategies that the complexities underlying carrying out the activity are overlooked by the teacher and also that the 'one-off' occasion takes on too much significance. In the examples above, a child may have difficulty with the task for a whole variety of reasons and further observation in different contexts over time may be needed to find out what the problem is. Or it may just have been a bad day. Nevertheless, such strategies have some place in establishing the range of capability and understanding across the class and can help the teacher to match activity to child more precisely.

REVIEWING WORK DONE

At the end of a piece of work the teacher will review the work with the child. This can be done in discussion with individuals or a group, but attention needs to be given to *each* child's work as an individual matter. Performing or composing work will be listened to either live or on tape. Listening and appraising work will be in written or spoken form, perhaps with pictures, or notation of movement. Discussion might be based on:

- starting points, musical aims and purposes;
- saying what has actually been done, describing the music, talk, dance, etc.;
- listing skills, knowledge and understanding displayed;
- saying what has actually been learnt and where it might lead.

It may not be possible to carry out a detailed discussion on every piece of work, but a pattern of review should be established and carried out at intervals. If children get used to a framework such as this they can begin to gain understanding and confidence in evaluating their own learning. Children should always carry out some direct self-assessment. The following two sentence completions can be used by the children at the end of any piece of work:

'*In this work I was able to . . .*'

'*I think I could now go on to . . .*'

When children have been working on a group task, individual self-assessment is important as a means of gaining a perspective on each child's experiences and learning.

A certain amount of work should be saved through the year. For younger children the teacher may need to manage this, though pupils can decide what is to be saved. With older children a practical way is to issue each child with a ten- or twenty-minute cassette tape on which to save chosen pieces of work. Children can also keep a music diary recording music composed, performed and listened to. Entries are dated and include factual information about the work and a review section in which children evaluate the music and include self-assessments of their learning. Tape and diary can be kept in a folder together with music notations. Reviewing work in music is the means by which the teacher can assess a child's capabilities and needs in music carefully enough to provide a basis for *matching* activity to child or to the range within a group of class.

REVIEWING PROGRESS OVER TIME

There will be points at which it will be valuable for the teacher to review a child's progress over the longer term and assess how things are developing. These points will arise out of the ordinary teaching situation, arriving at a point with a child where there is a need to take stock and consider future action. They will also arise where reporting to parents, record-keeping, End of Key Stage Descriptions or points of transfer make it necessary to have a clear picture of how learning has progressed over a stretch of time. This review will be two-sided, drawing on both the teacher's assessment and the child's own self-assessment. The latter is crucial to a child's understanding of what music learning involves; it may also give valuable pointers to where work should lead next.

The practicality of this depends on the teacher being clear about how music fits into the whole approach to assessment and record-keeping for the class. If work in music is regularly reviewed as above, and very brief records kept, then reviewing progress over a term or half-year is much easier. This might take the form of a few minutes spent with the child tracing how music work has developed and going through the work saved. A framework such as the one suggested on page 66 which outlines five areas of *building* in music is a useful basis for longer-term review. The information is then readily available when children's general profiles are to be completed or reports made. Ritchie (1991) discusses ways of compiling the child's profile, including musical examples. All such reviews should have an element of looking forward in them. Agreeing an outline future learning plan in which teacher and child set targets helps the child to have a clearer view of his or her learning and self as a 'music person'.

In summary, assessment must be seen as an ongoing part of the teaching process, necessary in order to:

- monitor a child's acquisition of skills, knowledge and understanding;
- interact effectively with the child in a learning situation;
- match activities to children's abilities and needs;
- provide for progression in the longer term;
- report on the child's learning.

Children should be involved in the assessment process and encouraged to develop the capacity to reflect upon their own learning.

REPORTING

In order to assess and report on children's learning, it is necessary to have some kind of framework to refer to. The National Curriculum for England and Wales provided this through its system of ten levels of attainment for each attainment target. The original curriculum working groups for art, music and physical education had specified ten calibrated levels of attainment, as for all other subjects (DES and Welsh Office, 1991a,b,c). However, even at that time there was a growing awareness of the overloading of the National Curriculum and its assessment and the number of 'level' assessments' which teachers were going to have to make was looking prodigious. The ten levels were, therefore, deleted by the then Secretary of State, Kenneth Clarke, in the interests of simplification and they did not appear in the final curriculum orders. Instead, presumably because of their lowly status in the curriculum, art, music and physical education had only a single End of Key Stage Description for each of the two attainment targets. These described 'the type and range of performance that the majority of pupils should characteristically demonstrate by the end of the key stage' and were intended 'to help teachers judge the extent to which their pupils' attainment relates to this expectation' (DFE, 1995, p. 8).

In effect, however, even End of Key Stage Descriptions implied assessment of attainment against levels of some kind and the absence of explicit levels left teachers to set out their own frameworks, with little guidance forthcoming concerning national expectations until key stage exemplification materials were produced by the Schools Curriculum and Assessment Authority (SCAA, 1997).

End of Key Stage Descriptions indicated the range of experiences children should have had and added tentative indicators characterizing how they should approach them; for example, it was expected at Key Stage 1 that children 'sing ... and play ... with confidence', and at Key Stage 2 that they 'perform accurately and confidently' and 'make expressive use of the musical elements' (DFE, 1995, p. 9). Yet the descriptions were remarkably lacking in clear expectations of skill attainment, quality of imagination and response, or extent of knowledge and understanding. This could be regarded as beneficial in allowing expectations to clarify as the widespread teaching of music took on some consistency. It could also be regarded as a drawback in omitting to set any but the most basic expectations of children taking part in musical activity.

Reporting on music in a way which is useful and informative for children, parents and teachers receiving children on transfer requires an awareness of the development of children's skills, knowledge, understanding and creativity and an alertness to each child's progress in relation to these. So, for example, a statement about a child's singing might include comment on skills of controlling timbre and dynamics, pitching, breath control and diction, a qualitative description of the child's musical expressiveness in singing, and some assessment of the child's understanding of the choices involved in interpreting a song.

In the end, the ease with which a teacher is able to report in this way on each child is closely related to the effectiveness with which assessment has been incorporated into the full sequence of planning and teaching. More than this, if the assessment agenda has been an explicit part of all teaching and if children have been expected consistently to make their own self-assessments against clearly identified criteria as a regular part of each session, aided by feedback from the teacher, the picture for reporting will be clearly in focus.

Both teachers and children need to be clear about the learning targeted in any particular activity. If work then proceeds with these objectives in mind, if teacher and children work together on difficulties which arise and explicitly discuss ways of making progress, if children's work is jointly listened to and reviewed, and if strategies for tracking progress are appropriately lightweight but effective, then the final stage of reporting becomes very straightforward.

References

Czerniewska, P. (1988) Reflections on writing. *Times Educational Supplement*, 4 March.

DES and Welsh Office (1991a) *Art for Ages 5–16*. London: HMSO.

DES and Welsh Office (1991b) *Physical Education for Ages 5–16*. London: HMSO.

DES and Welsh Office (1991b) *Music for Ages 5–16*. London: HMSO.

DFE (1995) *Music in the National Curriculum*. London: HMSO.

Ritchie, R. (ed.) (1991) *Profiling in Primary Schools: A Handbook for Teachers*. London: Cassell.

School Curriculum and Assessment Authority (SCAA) (1997) *Expectations in Music at Key Stages 1 and 2*. London: SCAA.

CHAPTER 5
Music in the Classroom at Key Stage 1
Lesley Flash

Introduction

Now and again in a normal week there are times of magic in the infant classroom. There seems to be a spark of spontaneous understanding between children and teacher, which is more than the words or the action of the moment, when preparation, presentation, mood and timing coincide to perfection. There are sometimes long intervals of luminescent peace when the teacher can observe every child co-operative and absorbed in whatever s/he may be doing. The more there is music the more frequent these times of magic become, because in music they happen repeatedly as part of the music itself. The more music is integrated with the rest of the work of the day the more the influence extends itself into all areas of the curriculum. Music becomes, not a separate item, but as easy and familiar a way of expressing and communicating ideas as language, mathematics and art.

The basic principles can be broken down into concepts simple enough for any teacher and the children to grasp. At each stage progression becomes the logical extension of the work already done. Working exactly along the lines of early years practice, in a combination of free play, shared exploration and didactic intervention, any teacher can become as easy with music as s/he feels with handwriting or basic number. Once an outline approach has been defined and the classroom organized to provide for the work, music activities can easily be incorporated into a topic or a plan for the day.

Introducing the elements of music

This section gives a series of *teacher-led* activities which engage children with the basic elements of music. The activities are designed:

- to help teachers and children to be involved together in a practical way with music;
- to help teachers to focus children's musical experiences in a way that helps them to build their understanding.

By isolating the elements of music and presenting them in this form,

74

children become familiar with basic musical skills and thinking which they can use in their vocal, instrumental, movement and listening work. The elements of music introduced below are:

- silence;
- timbre;
- duration and rhythm;
- pitch and melody;
- dynamics.

A short explanation of each of the musical elements is included. Before playing the games with children they can be played with colleagues and friends and might also provide possible workshop experiences in an inservice day.

Whatever the age of the children, if little class-time has previously been devoted to music it will be necessary to begin with the simplest activities. The older the children, the more rapidly they will move onwards, but by starting from basics the teacher will be able to establish a music-profile of the class and help them to progress step by step. The activities can all be included as part of a normal day in the early years classroom. The activities can be seen as *games* and are intended to inform through enjoyment. Like any other primary school activity they are intended first to provide the experience and subsequently to become the subject of discussion. Games have the advantage of isolating and making central a particular element of music which might otherwise be difficult to distinguish in the participant's experience of music as a whole. Some games will need to be played many times and in several variations before the teacher feels that the children have an area of experience and skill sufficiently broad for them to be able to identify the common central notion.

Whenever more than two or three take part in an activity together it is worth taking turns for one of the number to be *a listener*. It is not that an audience is necessary to validate music-making, but that the comments of a listener, and the experience of listening, are useful when experimenting. The discussions that are provoked help to examine the processes involved and to identify them by agreed names if not by the 'proper' ones.

SILENCE

The silence was measured at intervals by the abrupt, melancholic hooting of a bird.

(Norman Lewis, *The Missionaries*)

Silence games make a good beginning. The function of silence, which is involved in all aspects of music, should be regarded as a positive quality without which music itself would have no force. The aim is to make the control of sound a matter of pride and excitement. The respect for the quality of the aural environment which this encourages and the discipline it requires prepare the way for later music games.

> Take ten very slow, very deep abdominal breaths counting on the in-breath 'and' and on the out-breath 'one', 'two', etc. Concentrate on the breathing and the counting. After 'ten' sit quietly and listen to silence.
>
> The children *hold a silence*. It may need to be pointed out to them that silent is different from quiet and that almost all movement makes a noise, so that if they are to be silent they will also need to be still. With young children it helps to have a visible measure of time such as a sand timer.
>
> Sit in silence with eyes closed. One person strikes an instrument. A metal or stringed instrument is easiest but any instrument will do. All listen. When the sound has completely died away the instrument is struck again.
>
> Sit in silence. Eyes can be open. One person claps a short pattern. The group thinks the pattern through in their heads and then repeats it. Do this several times using the same pattern or different ones.

With the youngest children it is worth placing emphasis on starting and stopping games in the hall. This will act as a form of physical reinforcement and patterning. With all ages it is important to keep in mind the possible parallel activities that can be planned for movement sessions.

> The children move as an instrument sounds and stop when the sound stops. The sound could be a tambour and the children can be encouraged over a period of time to match their movement to the rhythm and speed of the sound. If the chosen sound is more ringing – a triangle, a cymbal or a chime bar – the children can be encouraged to move just one part of their body and stop when they can no longer hear the sound.

TIMBRE

Timbre (pronounced '*tambra*') is the peculiar and variable quality of any sound. The way in which the voice or an instrument is used affects the characteristic tone and produces differing responses in the hearer. Games to explore sound quality and the manipulation of sound will develop out of games with silence as one of the next natural steps.

Play a drum or a tambour with different parts of the hand, or collect a selection of beaters and listen to their different effects. Listen to them played at different speeds or in different rhythms. Some may be better for some purposes than others. Try the same rhythm on several different sorts of instrument or on all the available varieties of one instrument. Compare and contrast.

Try identifying an instrument, and how it is played, unseen from behind a screen. Try identifying people, unseen, by their voices repeating a common phrase or singing a song.

Many ideas for games occur as the teacher listens 'out of the corner of the ear' to what goes on in the music corner or elsewhere in the classroom. A discovery made by one child may be worth commending to all the children. A collection of metallic sounds played by one child as a sequence could inspire others to make a pattern of metallic sounds or a sequence of a different collection of sound-types. New techniques may make themselves obvious or can be encouraged.

Talking about timbre with children soon leads into the realms of simile, poetry and invented language. To have some agreed onomato-poeic nonsense words or descriptive phrases can be useful in the beginning. A rewarding conversation can be held with four-year-olds about 'squeaky-eee' sounds and 'cooee-ooo' tones where talking about 'shrill' and 'mellow' would be meaningless. The language used will develop with the children and become richer with their experience and helps with their growing awareness about language. The teacher will also notice greater discrimination in the choices they make in their own music.

DURATION, RHYTHM

Duration is the length of time that an individual sound lasts. *Rhythm* is the ebb and flow of the music. It can include a regular pattern but it is not exclusively a measurable quality. Working with a pulse is a necessary part of rhythm work but it is not the whole. Always trying to impose a steady beat runs the risk of inhibiting the children's intuitive rhythmic response which is more wide-ranging.

77

The *pulse* is the steps the music takes.

> Try saying, to a regular pulse: 'sound, silence, sound, silence, sound, silence.'
>
> Now repeat the exercise but think the word 'silence' and say only the word 'sound'.
>
> Repeat, thinking 'sound' and saying 'silence'. When the underlying measure of sound or silence is an equal length of time, then there is a steady beat.

Metre is the shape which the grouping of beats in twos, threes, fours, etc. gives to the music as some beats take on more emphasis than others.

There is much that can be done in music, especially in group work, once the children can keep a steady beat at varying paces, but the process cannot be hurried. The level of complexity in the games will depend on the skill of the children and this is partly a question of maturation. On the whole, the younger the children the better off they are using hands rather than instruments and beaters, and tapping rather than clapping. Clapped hands tend to stick together, but two fingers bounced lightly on the opposite palm, or finger tips on heads, arms or floor, work well. Throwing the upturned hands both outwards for a silent beat maintains the body rhythm without hiatus.

> Try 'tap, tap, out: tap, tap, out' for 'sound, sound, silent: sound, sound, silent'. This gives a feeling of 'three' as a metre.

At any age there is a thrill in the whole group playing *rhythm patterns* together. When the teacher initiates the activity it is important to be content with simple accuracy when it happens and approximate accuracy when it doesn't. It is better to find as many different ways as possible to re-invent the best the children can do and to introduce new work gradually than to press too far, too fast, and to make rhythm-work or any other work in music a bore and a chore. Rhythm patterns should be felt and played together until they are as easy as talking. They can lapse inter-changeably into language or movement.

Once the children are in the habit of responding, whether it be to copy, reply to, invent or read a pattern, they are games that anyone can start. A pattern tapped out with a spoon in the sand-tray may be picked up by another child building with bricks, and another pausing during colouring-in and tapping with the crayon, and another swinging the feet whilst reading, until some or all of the class are playing. A pattern may be invented for a particular musical context, such as accompanying a song, or taken from something heard in the listening session which really appealed.

Find rhythms based on word patterns. Play them over and over, listening to the sounds.

Make up a rhythm pattern. Tap it, think it, tap it.

One claps patterns for the rest to echo. Include one pattern which must not be copied (as in 'Simon says').

One plays a rhythm pattern. They look at another person who copies or answers, then looks at another who copies or answers, and so on.

Make rhythm patterns which include silent beats. In pairs, one plays a pattern over and over again. The partner plays in the silent beats so that the two patterns interlock.

More rhythm pattern activities can be carried out using *rhythm-pattern cards*. These introduce a simple notation system so that children can match sound to symbol as they practise the patterns. Children find it easiest to read notation for beats as single marks. Conventional music notation should be introduced only very gradually as the children become obviously ready to learn it. Start by using the skeletal version, as follows:

Whole beat:

|

Two half-beats:

⊓

Rest:

Z

Steady beat of three whole beats:

| | |

Rhythm pattern based on three whole beats:

| Z ⊓

Rhythm pattern based on three whole beats:

⊓ ⊓ |

Steady beat of five whole beats:

| | | | |

Rhythm pattern based on five whole beats:

⊓ | | ⊓ |

This flows easily into standard musical notation by adding the 'dots' later.

It is perfectly possible to make a piece of music or movement with *no steady beat.*

Play three or more sounds at random on an instrument or two, choosing sounds that promise to be interesting. After the first sound, play the second sound when feeling dictates and so with however many sounds are played. If the music pleased, play it again. It probably won't sound exactly the same but that doesn't matter. Experiment a little.

Make a sequence of three or four movements. For the sake of demonstration try, as separate postures, a floor-level shape, a middle-level lateral shape, and a different floor-level shape. Then repeat them but find a way for each to flow into the next. Practise the sequence. Try to vary the duration of each pose and the speed of the flow between them.

In the case of both the music and the movement there is a piece of work that is rhythmic, though not in the sense of having a regular pulse. Although the work does have its own internal structural tensions they vary according to the way the quality of the whole is developed.

PITCH AND MELODY

Melody is the line and shape of music as it moves higher and lower through pitch 'space'. The concept of pitch, of 'higher and lower than' is one that children take time to absorb. During Key Stage 1 they are still developing the ability to pitch accurately with their voices.

Hum a note. Keep the same *pitch*. Let all the children listen and then join in as they can find it. Keep taking breaths as needed!

When everyone has joined in let the sound fade gradually into silence. (This game can be used at any time to get children's attention and gather them together.)

Next, move the note to another pitch and let the children, after listening, join in with the next note, and so on.

Take a short fragment of a well-known song. Sing it and think about the *shape* as it moves up and down. Think about what the voice was doing to produce the sounds. Think it through and sing it again. Sing it once more using large gestures drawn in the air to show the directions the voice was taking.

Take a second song and repeat the game. How do the two *phrases* differ? How was the voice moving? Use words such as jump, step, leap, slide, swoop. What variety was there?

Just as rhythm patterns can be notated using the simple system described above, so melodic shapes can be written down in ways that will lead easily into standard musical notation.

This might begin as:

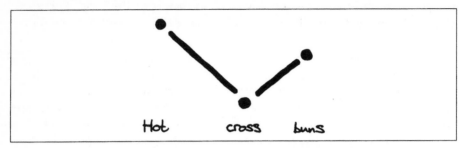

and develop into:

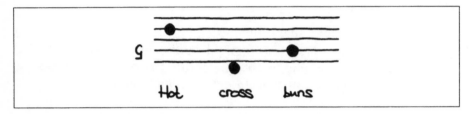

This method can then be brought together with the rhythm symbols towards the standard notation.

DYNAMICS

Dynamics are the drama of music, the loud and soft, and all points in between.

> From utter silence start a steady beat and let it rise extremely slowly to the loudest sound that can be made. Drop it suddenly to the softest sound and repeat. End in a silence as long as the music was. Reverse the process.
>
> Invent as many ways as possible of getting from loud to soft and vice versa.

Dynamics is initially a simple subject for class-work. Children soon develop the control necessary to manipulate and sustain exciting tensions between the contrasting opposites. These contrasts are easy to identify and have great appeal but this is not to say that they are the only factors of dramatic force that children can appreciate. Is the piece which gets louder and faster (typical of children's early work) exciting because of the dynamics or the tempo or both? Playing with the range of each element, and the elements combined, produces new work with different force.

One child starts and keeps a steady beat. Another joins in and drops out, keeping the same beat, as she feels like it. Try it again with more people. Each maintain consistent volume if possible.

Start and keep a steady beat at a constant volume. A friend drops in and out, keeping the same beat, at whatever varying volume she pleases, using whatever instruments she likes.

Select a combination of four or five instruments that sound good together. Somebody begin. The rest join in and drop out as they feel, playing what variations of rhythm, volume and style each wishes.

LEADING MUSIC ACTIVITIES

The teacher's method of presentation in music games requires some preparatory thought. Too much explanation before starting can be deadening and, to younger children, unintelligible. If the teacher establishes from the outset clear guiding signals for starting and stopping and some of the simpler changes such as getting louder/softer and faster/slower the game can be started with a few introductory words and then guided by gesture. As time goes on, and the more responsive to one another the children and the teacher become, the less overt 'leading' is necessary and the child may be able to take over.

Planning for music

Planning for music requires above all that music should be expected to be an inseparable part of daily class life. The following section will consider the teacher's planning for music. Music events happen during the flow of classroom life. All curriculum subjects require planning, and so does music. But music for young children is slightly different. Rather than set *lessons* there should be a trickle effect, where the teacher introduces short activities and then children are able to repeat and practise them individually or in groups. If the teacher is going to introduce a substantial activity with the whole class then it is necessary to choose the right moment in the week and this might be any time. It is better not to fix a time ahead.

During Key Stage 1 children should have the opportunity to discover a wide range of vocal and instrumental sounds and to sing, play and improvise freely. They should have been able to listen to and discuss music from many sources, including not least their own invented music. They should have been given the opportunity to experience music as part

83

of their lives through games, dance and song and have been enabled to respond in a variety of ways.

Songs, games or a listening-time can be planned for any time between two to twenty minutes, at intervals or all at once, during the course of the day. In the classroom the music corner will be available for individual choosing and directed activity and on most days there will be hall-times that can be used for movement work, improvisation and whole-class instrumental work.

In order to preserve flexibility, but at the same time to maintain some structure and development, the use of a system of cards by the teacher and the children is recommended. When writing out the daily plan it is useful to have a way in which to note down the details of activities. A teacher's plan for the morning may look like Figure 1.

A more detailed teacher's card for music is shown in Figure 2. This

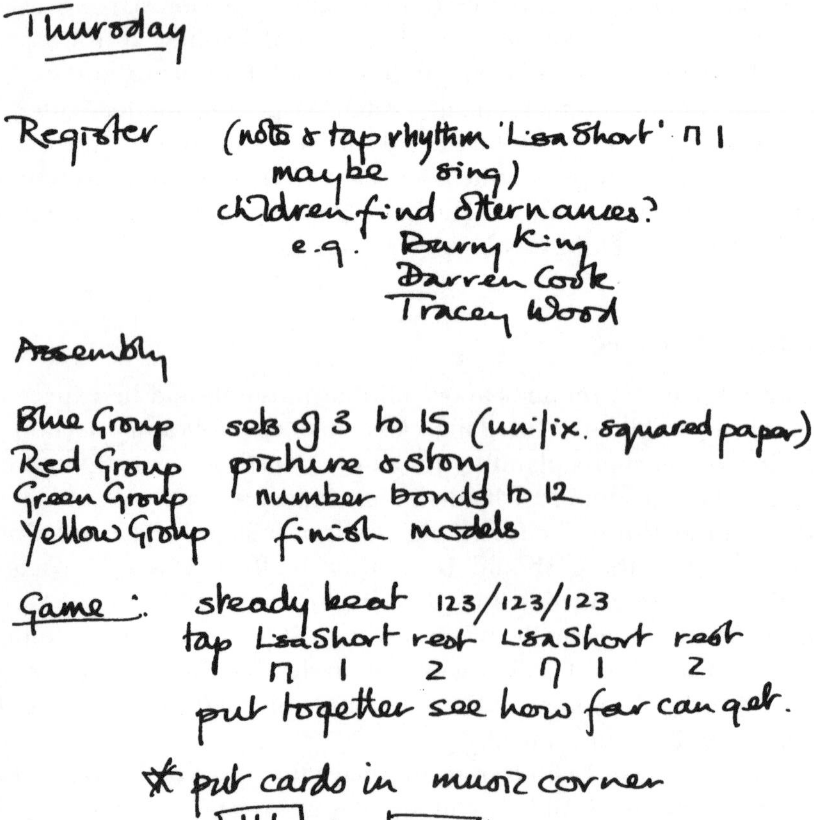
Thursday

Register (note & tap rhythm 'Lisa Short' ⊓ | maybe sing)
children find other names?
e.g. Barry King
Darren Cook
Tracey Wood

Assembly

Blue Group sets of 3 to 15 (unifix. squared paper)
Red Group picture & story
Green Group number bonds to 12
Yellow Group finish models

Game: steady beat 123/123/123
tap Lisa Short rest Lisa Short rest
⊓ | 2 ⊓ | 2
put together see how far can get.

* put cards in music corner
| | | & ⊓ | 2 ? | ⊓ 2

Figure 1

Game: Sets of Three
No. 8 : Sets of Three with
        Name Patterns.

You need: Two people, or two groups,
        and a listener

Keep a steady beat 123, making 1 a
strong beat. Choose a name with
2 half-beats and a whole beat.
[ta-te taa]... (⊓ I). Put a rest at the
end (ta-te taa rest) ... (⊓ I z). Put
the two patterns together. Start
with the steady beat to guide you.

I I I I I I I I I I I I I I I I I I I I I I
     ⊓ I z ⊓ I z ⊓ I z ⊓ I z ⊓ I z

What else can you do with patterns
of three?

Figure 2

card, if used with children, leaves scope for invention according to their
interests and abilities. They might choose other names which would fit
into 3 whole beats, or put a tune to the game, or use instruments or
patterns of other numbers.

Cards for children and the teacher to use together might look like
Figure 3. The class will have learned this song together and the card is
kept in the music corner for the children to use by themselves.

Initially the teacher will find that cards can be made as work develops.
It becomes clear which activities are most inspiring and cards can be
added, discarded or re-structured. Children will often take the music
cards as starting points in a general choosing session in the classroom.

Diddle diddle dumpling

My son John

Went to bed

With his trousers on....

Figure 3

Younger children may seem to go wildly off at tangents, but the intention is there and should be respected as the thing itself; older children are more likely to begin as suggested and then to develop something of their own. Not all games will translate readily into a pictured or written form suitable for the class.

Following the early games, the first cards should be introduced to help children practise their skill. Once the children clearly recognize the meaning of each mark from their own experience of the games, any new cards can be shown before being played, as a challenge to their skill.

Voices, singing and song-making

VOICE GAMES

In the early days of making music with the children it is important to emphasize the use of the voice as a conscious instrument in sound games and sound-and-silence games. Any child can play the voice. It need not even be in song.

> Play games to identify different voices, both the different sorts of voices that can be used such as singing, talking, shouting, whispering and the voices of hidden individuals.
>
> The children take a given sound 'for a walk'. The sound can be single – ooo – or multiple – mmmoooowwch – and the stops, starts, ups and downs, swoops, jumps and changes in volume can be indicated by the teacher's hand.

Voice-sounds can be used instead of, or as well as, instruments in a class game.

> In two groups, with a third group listening, tap a steady beat and a ⊓ | rhythm pattern together.
>
> One person keep the beat on a tambour, everybody tap the pattern.
>
> Everybody keep the beat, one person beat the pattern on a tambour.
>
> One person tap the beat *very* lightly on a tambour, everybody else tap the pattern on their shoulders.
>
> One person clap or keep the beat, everybody else chant 'Oo ahah oo ahah oo ahah'.
>
> One group chant the beat as 'O, O, O', one group chant 'Oo ahah', and so on.

There could be several groups (one listening).

> In three groups, chant the beat as 'Hey' and 'Ho' and the pattern as 'Ha hee-hee'.
>
> In three groups, chant the beat as 'Tea' and the pattern as 'Cake biscuit' and 'Jam jelly'.

The next game introduces a drone which is an addition to the original game.

> In four groups, chant the beat as 'Tea' and the pattern as 'Cake biscuit' and 'Jam jelly' and the fourth group hum continuously 'Mmmmmmmm'.

Varying the texture and the dynamics of the same games makes something else that is 'the same yet different' or 'similar but not the same' – both in themselves useful phrases in conversation about music.

> Choose any of the above and, in each group, starting one group at a time, bring in each individual voice one after the other. Either fade out one at a time or stop all at once.
>
> Choose any one of the above and all players drop in and out at will but there must never be a silence until an agreed number of beats after full chorus has been reached.
>
> Choose any one of the above and vary the volume and intensity of the sounds, either as a full chorus, or as each group having its own role, or playing at will within an agreed plan. Reaching certain levels could be used as a signal from one group to another, to join in, drop out or change.

There are opportunities for developing impromptu voice games in many children's stories. The teacher's skill in telling can highlight conscious voice effects, while many stories for younger children have refrains, chants and jingles that can be copied or slightly changed and used as music games. Some will be best as rhythmic spoken games, which may slide into a chant, while others will be suitable for putting to a known or newly invented tune.

PITCHING VOICES

Young children's singing voices are neither so flexible nor so high as required by many of the songs they are asked to sing. The teacher's own voice may not necessarily easily adapt itself to the range of which the children are capable. Individual teachers have different ranges of singing voice but the development of children's voices can be encouraged even by those teachers who are shy of their own voices or who find it difficult to adapt to a child's range. The teacher may have reservations about his/her own voice as a model for the children. But there is no reason not to try to develop the voice by working with the children at a simple level, and allow the children to comment and encourage this development.

Voice-sound-matching Sound-matching timbre games can be extended into pitch work. Voice-matching round a circle, in which one person starts a sung sound and the rest join in on or near the same note, is the simplest game to begin with. Keep taking breaths as needed and concentrate all attention on just keeping the note steady.

> Ask a child to sort and match a small selection of chime bars, and then to try matching his/her own voice to one of the notes played. It is best to start with no more than two pairs for sorting, and to make a big ceremony out of careful striking of the note, listening attentively to the sound, and stopping the vibrations with the thumb or finger before trying the next note or speaking.

Matching the note with the voice is more a question of how it feels most comfortable to do it. Some feel happier matching the note while it still sounds. Gradually extend to several notes with mastery of each stage.

Ear and voice It is well worth introducing singing activities which use only a limited number of notes. These are intended to develop the accurate pitch of the voice, starting first from the natural falling call or the 'coo-ee' that everybody uses without thinking. This is the relation between the notes G and E, or F and D (a minor third). Hand signs can be used in conjunction with the voice to indicate the movement of the sound. Given that the development of ear and voice for pitch is gradual and that the work goes by in slow simple stages, this is where the teacher can join in and try to develop his/her own voice along with the children.

> Choose the chime bars G and E. Strike the G and match voices to it. Sing the note without the instrument, choosing an open sound such as 'naa'. Then use the E in the same way. Next make patterns of the two notes and sing them, listening very carefully to match the voices to the chime bars' notes. Start with a pattern of falling from G to E.

Use hand gestures to help the children visualize the movement. (Other notes with the same *interval* can be used: C and A, D and B.)

Simple copying and dialogue, guided by the teacher, can follow, using the notes already introduced, for example on G–E:
    Copying:
        Teacher signs and sings: Hello (G–E)
        Teacher signs and child sings: Hello (G–E)
    Dialogue:
        Teacher signs and sings: Hello (G–E) How are you? (G–G–E)
        Child sings: Very well (E–E–G)

As the children become adept they will invent and sign their own patterns and songs. Using the children's own names in sol-fa games is a very easy way to begin personal song-making. Little songs can be made on no more than two or three notes and invention in the music corner can be encouraged by putting out only the appropriate chime-bars. Children will invent songs as part of their developmental play.

It is a good idea to work with the relationship between two notes for a while to become familiar with the interval. The combination of activity for ear, eye and body impresses the music on the children. Provided the work is undertaken little and often and always for fun then during the course of their years in the infant school there is no reason why the children should not achieve several notes accurately pitched.

No early years teacher ignores the importance to a child of his/her own name. They can be used as rhythm patterns, inserted in songs, and turned into songs in their own right:

'David, Khalid, Caroline, Claire'

Regularly repeated class instructions can, in the same way, be fitted into limited pitch tunes, such as shown in Figure 4.

don't run......walk don't shout....talk

Figure 4

This idea can also be used with the tunes of well-known songs. A simple example could be, to the tune of 'Boys and girls go out to play':

Children, please put your work away.
It's half-past-ten and time to play!
Pick up the pencils and tuck in the chairs.
Find your partner and line up in pairs.

SINGING

Singing relieves stress. There is plenty of that, of even the happiest kind, in a classroom. Whether it is the result of momentary social unity, the controlled breathing or the vibration of the nerves, a good sing can be wonderfully uplifting. Far better that it should be simple fun than that it should become a source of agony and exposure. With young children the simplest of songs in the shortest of repertoires can be used and re-used to make something different. The reworking of the familiar provides variety and challenge in an area of security and makes any musical point more easily accessible.

A sample follows of the ways in which a familiar song can be used for song activities which explore rhythm and structure:

Pease Porridge Hot

Remember to have a listener group as well.

Sing it once:

Pease porridge hot
Pease porridge cold
Pease porridge in the pot
Nine days old.

Sing it twice and at the end sing and clap the phrase 'Nine days old'.

3 groups: one sing 'Pease porridge hot', one sing 'Pease porridge cold', one sing 'Pease porridge in the pot', and all sing and clap 'Nine days old.'

2 groups: one sing (or sing and clap) 'Nine days old' throughout the song while the other sings the song through.

As above but the first group just claps.

As above but use 'Pease porridge hot' as the continuous refrain.

As above but use 'Pease porridge hot' and 'Nine days old' as two continuous refrains.

Clap the two refrains and the whole song, all together.

2 groups: one sings 'Hot' or 'Cold' in tune all the way though as a steady beat while the other group sings the song.

2 groups: one sings 'Hot, cold, hot, cold' in tune as a continuous refrain while the other group sings the song.

And so on.

Other songs may not be as suitable for as many variations as this example but most songs offer something. One great advantage of this approach is that the children can appreciate the changes as something which they themselves have made rather than trying to discover differences in something that already has the sound of seamless whole.

While singing children can be helped to become aware of the use of their voices for phrasing and style:

Talk with the children about:
How do they need to use their breath to control and direct the flow of the song? Which songs require explosive energy and which require slow release? How do they control the loudness and softness? How do they need to articulate the words to get the best effect? A group of listeners is very important in these discussions.

The teacher of early years children must bear in mind that, although s/he will be able to feel much of how best the song can be sung, the children will not necessarily be able to sing it even as clearly as they can comment on it. Straining to produce a perfect choir will exhaust everybody and depress the children.

Little and often in activity and discussion, contentment with the simplest form of success and pleasure, endless capacity for surprise and delight, and preparedness to be led by the children are golden rules for working with music. The voice is the one instrument available to all at any time. Singing just for joy should never be lost in the classroom.

> The man that hath no music in himself,
> Nor is not moved with concord of sweet sounds,
> Is fit for treasons, stratagems, and spoils.
> The motions of his spirit are dull as night,
> And his affections dark as Erebus.
> Let no such man be trusted. Mark the music.
>   (William Shakespeare, *The Merchant of Venice*, Act 5, Sc. 1)

COMPOSING SONGS

Children compose their own songs spontaneously and naturally, and these can be quite subtle and sophisticated in their musical use of rhythm, melody, inflection and structure. They show how much the child has already absorbed from previous song-singing experiences. The teacher needs to listen for this, especially when the children are playing, encourage it and provide situations where it can flourish. During circle time, or class time, the teacher can invite children to offer a song they have made up, or to make one up on the spot. Music-corner play can often result in songs being made with or without instrumental accompaniment. A facility for tape-recording children's singing can help to catch the music as it happens. This allows the child, and other children, to hear and review the song and it can be included in a profile of the child's musical development. (See Chapter 7 for more discussion of children's song composition.)

CHOOSING SONGS

Children should sing a variety of songs from a wide range of cultural traditions. In choosing songs it is important to bear in mind the *musical elements* in the song. Songs can give children experiences of different rhythm patterns, melodic features, dynamic possibilities and voice quality. Songs should also offer a range of musical styles and moods which reflect different cultures and use of the singing voice: in a boat song, in a street cry, in a religious context or in a pop idiom.

Much good material is now available and there are some suggested sources at the end of this book. When a song has been chosen it is important to listen to how the children manage it to make sure that it is within their range and capability. Collections of children's songs sometimes include material which is unsuitable in these ways, although the title might be attractive.

Music and movement

Music and movement can reflect and reinforce one another. Movement has the great advantage of involving the whole body, and so the whole being, of the child. The young child is so much the centre of his or her own universe, so much an undifferentiated force of the senses, thought and feeling, that the response to music is as much physical as emotional or intellectual. Thought, mood and action are one.

Reference has already been made to the way in which movement activities in the hall can be linked to early work in sound and silence.

Simple invented sequences, patterns and tunes can be played to accompany sequences and patterns of movement. Ring-games, country-dance and action-songs or rhymes are ways of exercising pattern, phrase and rhythm. The one exemplifies the other, whether or not the teacher chooses to make the connection explicit. In some cases the connection becomes clear to the children only after several days or weeks of repeating a particular sort of activity. The moment when a child says 'Oh yeah! It's like ... ' is the moment when the teacher knows s/he has succeeded.

Music and movement can be in response to other learning:

Suppose that the children have been working on a sequence of movement such as making a strong shape at different levels. The emphasis behind the work will have been less on 'strong' and 'move' – which could tempt the use of a lot of loud, heavy, thumping music – than on effort and the pivot of balance – which would suggest music with a slow development to climax and a sudden fall.

Suppose that work on reflecting patterns has been involving the children in music, then work on reflecting movement could take place in the hall. Music need not necessarily accompany it. The emphasis behind the work would be on the nature of reflecting – mirror images, symmetry, reversal, simple copying or distortion. A literal parallel need not be drawn. If the work is well done then the ideas will connect one with another in time.

A spring-term topic on frogs and tadpoles may have led to work in the hall on jumps and leaps. The children will have been jumping at different heights, in different directions, while travelling in different directions and with different ways of landing and taking off. In music this could have led to all sorts of work with jumps in sound movement, not just in pitch, but in tempo, timbre, dynamics, rhythms. Ultimately, depending on the age of the class, work in both areas might have come together in a drama activity.

Provided the teacher is prepared to *look beyond the literal* there is almost no end to the creative possibilities in music in the curriculum. The question that the teacher needs to ask is 'What is the sound or the movement *doing?*' as if it had an existence of its own without human agency. A similar question needs to be asked when working with children's instrumental music.

Instruments, improvising and composing

EXPLORING INSTRUMENTS

Few children have the opportunity to play a variety of sound-makers before they come to school and there needs to be a period of exploration before attempting to discuss any sort of intention or structure with the player. It takes time for the teacher to get to know individuals and what can be expected and encouraged in each. Among the many virtues of music games is that music can be made in groups of varying sizes. The teacher can study the children while playing the game. With an overview of the capabilities of the children it is possible to encourage free experimentation in the music area. This will take place alongside the common experience of basic elements of music which the children will have had through games.

Accommodating instrumental music for free play in the classroom is always possible if the teacher is firm about the parameters within which it is allowed to operate. If the class is well prepared to respect the quality of the aural environment through the playing of music games which emphasize the value of silence and the subtleties of sound, then they have made a head start. If, in the music games, the teacher has encouraged a careful interest in the qualities and the potential of the instruments used, then the behaviour will continue when the children are operating alone. Setting down rules for the treatment of instruments is essential and infringement should suffer instant sanctions. It is too easy to accept a level of noise and behaviour in children that, at an adult level, would constitute musical thuggery. It is not too much to ask the children to respect the presence of others about them.

Instruments can be introduced first to the whole class and then made available in the music corner.

In the music circle, pass round a new instrument (or its beater) asking each child to make a different sound. On the way children can describe the sound heard, try to copy the last sound, listen to the sound, think it in their heads, listen to it again, teach the next child how to make the sound.

Choose four or five instruments and find lots of sound made with them. Sort the sounds made into sets. The sets might be according to:

the action which makes the sound (blow, pluck, scrape, shake, strike);

the material producing the sound (wood, metal, skin, string);

> length, loudness, pitch, timbre.
>
> The children can invent their own sets.

It is worth giving some thought to the selection of instruments available at any one time. By changing the variety of beaters, choosing instruments made all of one type of material or played all in one particular way, or by making only a particular set of notes available on chime bars or xylophones, the teacher can channel the course that experimentation takes. Provision and selection of instruments in the music corner can focus experimentation in a particular area.

> Suppose the teacher wanted every child to have had experience of metal sounds. To this end the music corner is devoted to a selection of metal instruments and objects with perhaps a few made of other materials for contrast (drums made of metal, wood, skin, clay, etc). Activity cards are available, suggesting experiments possible with these instruments. Every child has been asked to spend some time there during the week.

CHILDREN PLANNING THEIR MUSIC

Some music will arise spontaneously out of improvisation and the spirit of the moment. Children can also be encouraged to plan their music, thinking beforehand about what they want to do.

> Errol's plan: 'It will go slow, slower and then *very* fast at the end, and I need two shakers and tambourines.'

It is possible to arrange with the children whose turn it will be and to ask them to give some thought to what they might like to do in the music corner the next day, even perhaps to make a note of it with someone at home. During the course of the following day each child has his or her turn. By giving previous thought to the matter, however young the child and however minimal the response may seem to an adult, the child has planned for music.

The teacher will ask to hear the results and, since there has been a statement of intent, both the teacher and the other children may comment as listeners. As the children become used to planning for music they will become at ease in discussing their work with their peers and the teacher. Music shared may be finished pieces or 'work in progress' and part of a process of thought.

> Two children had been making music for the plan that one of them had made. They came to play it for the other children. The music had a clear structure and strong rhythmic patterns and was full of dramatic effects. When the players had finished the children listening began to discuss the music without waiting for a word from the teacher.

The mood of a classroom can change. For the sake of all who work in the classroom it is justifiable occasionally to adjust the supply of instruments to those which feel right that day. There are days when drums are wonderful and days when they are not to be tolerated. If the children become used to planning all their work it also means that, when necessary, the music corner can be declared closed without fear of losing too much of the spontaneity that is of value in children's responses. An idea sounded out on one or two quieter instruments can serve as 'rough work'. The child and teacher can together make a few written or drawn notes of how the piece may go. When the corner again becomes available those notes will serve as a reminder.

It is worth limiting the numbers of children who may work in the music corner. In the early days one or two at a time is plenty but as the children's work in music develops some of them will want to work in larger groups. Again, if the children can plan and discuss their ideas with the teacher, they can defer the playing without disturbing children working in the class. Larger groups might go to the hall with a helper, work in the corridor, or come back to the classroom at lunch-time. Some children may wish to work alone and in peace. Provision can be made for them in a similar way.

CHILDREN 'SAVING' MUSIC

Tape-recording Providing the means for children to tape-record work if they wish to do so is useful. If the children can record their own work themselves they will lose the self-consciousness that comes from making recording 'an occasion' and they will begin to make choices about what and when they choose to record. Listening to their own work as an audience will encourage them to appraise it for themselves.

Tape-recording is also an excellent partial solution to the difficulties a teacher has in allocating time. It is not necessary to listen to everything a child plays and, indeed, the child may prefer to be private, but when the child does solicit it the teacher's response means a great deal. Promising to take home a tape of a child's music is a fair compromise if taping facilities are available and it is simply not possible to go to listen 'live'.

Tape-recording offers the benefit of being able to listen to a work several times.

Written recording A musical score is the written record of a piece of music. Conventional adult scores are far too dense for most young children and even in the simplest form should be presented gradually and with care only when the time is right.

Mention has already been made of various ways in which music can be represented symbolically without recourse to formal notation. The transition from representation by objects, such as beads or unifix, to symbols, such as squiggles and blocks of colour, and thence by degrees to formal notation is not necessarily a sequence of stages. Infant children may find none or all of these forms of representation useful at any one time. What is essential is that, when symbolization is appropriate, they should understand the agreed relationship between the music and the form of symbolization chosen.

In the same way that the teacher knows which of the multiple ways of helping a child to read is useful at a particular juncture, so the teacher who is sensitive to the way in which the class is developing musically will come know to when it is helpful to use symbolization and what form to use.

In the early years children do 'emergent writing'. Children will do the equivalent in music. Just as in emergent writing, where children grasp that there are certain symbols which are used to represent language, so they begin to learn that there are musical symbols which they begin to incorporate into their written repertoire. When they want to record their musical ideas, they should be helped to use similar forms of emergent music notation. Their early musical notation will be a combination of patterns used by the teacher, such as those on the rhythm cards, letter names seen on the instruments, and their own pictorial representations (see Figures 5, 6 and 7).

IDEAS FOR MUSIC

To extend music-corner work it is useful to have *suggestion cards* available, written along the lines of the cards illustrated earlier. They should each focus on as small an area of activity as possible for the initial stimulus and leave scope for development as wide as possible. It may help to make a note of ideas for extended activity on the back of each card as a reminder to the teacher. There may be a class helper who is prepared to act as a listener. This can be invaluable in the early days of introducing a music corner. The helper can sit beside the children, reading any card they

Figure 5

Figure 6

Figure 7

can't manage, offering a response, occasionally joining in, and acting as a model for the care of instruments. Some examples of suggestions for activity that can be pursued at any level of competence follow. Some are in two parts to suggest directions for development.

Make some music for wooden instruments/metal instruments/skins.

Make some music for wooden/metal/skin instruments that are shaken/struck/scraped.

....

Choose an instrument. Find out how many ways you can play it. Make a piece of music for all those ways.

Take the music you have just made and teach it to a friend. Ask your friend to make up a piece to go with your music.

....

Make a piece of music with a beginning, a middle and an end.

Make a piece of music with a beginning, a middle and an end. Make the end like the beginning and make the middle as different as can be.

....

Make some music with a friend with instruments you can play with your hands. Try the same music with sticks.

Find very, very quiet sounds on some instruments. Make a very, very quiet piece of music. Take your quiet music and let it get louder, very slowly.

Try making short sounds on an instrument. Try making short sounds on three different instruments. Put the sounds together in a piece of music.

Try different ways to play together:

- Try answering one another in music
- Try answering (friendly)
- Try answering (resisting)
- Try answering (copying)
- Try answering (echoing)
- Try answering (interrupting)
- Try answering (finishing each other's sentences)

Provided one begins from a sufficiently simple idea then there is almost no limit to the interpretations that can be put upon it. 'Some music for metal instruments' could be anything from a four-year-old on a triangle to a horn concerto.

The appearance of the music corner should encourage children's music-making. If paintings and drawings have been encouraged as a form of response to music then some of these can be used. Some children may have written about an aspect of music-making if not about the music itself. Others may have illustrated songs as a single picture or a sequence. Children may have made their own scores and be keen to display them in progress or completed. A larger score for an ongoing project or a listening enthusiasm may occupy the space for a while. Rhythm pattern cards could be occasionally displayed, as opposed to filed, in such a way that they could form a longer pattern if played as part of a game. The class song cards could be kept on the wall for a few weeks instead of in a box. Each display will encourage different directions in music.

WHOLE CLASS INSTRUMENTS

Using instruments for music with the whole class can be a challenge. If it is to be done, the teacher needs to have a clear idea of what he or she is going to do and how, and to have a very efficient system of distribution. The younger the children the longer this takes, with the attendant risk of losing their interest. If, on the other hand, the children have played so many music games that they are comfortable with voice parts and proud of them, and responsive and adept with clapping and tapping, as well as being able to be interested listeners, then the scale of the challenge is reduced. It is still necessary to have a clear plan but now there can be an audience, a voice section, a hand or foot section, and an instrumental section. Furthermore, the sections can be rotated. The class might try:

- rhythm and melody patterns built up layer by layer;
- following a plan: each group in turn, then all together;
- trying out a particular idea: music using echoes;
- making instrumental music to go with a song: before it begins, between verses, to end it, as an accompaniment.

PROVISION OF INSTRUMENTS

The selection of sound-makers made available to children deserves careful thought when the allocation of a budget is in question. Quality is important, but so also is suitability to age, stage and purpose.

Percussion instruments are essential. Generally the instruments which are shaken, struck or scraped are easiest for young children, who are still developing fine motor skills. There should be as much variety as it is possible to afford. There should also be a variety of instruments which can be plucked, bowed or blown. The rarer instruments can be circulated by agreement or kept centrally with a borrowing book. Lively music corners will in any event be constantly changing. Home-made instruments and sound-makers also have their uses but they should supplement the existing provision of good-quality manufactured instruments, not substitute for it. It is worth building up a class or school collection of such things as bowls or pots, large shells and seed-pods, seeds, bones and pieces of pipe, tube or rod and any other object which can be used to make a distinct and curious sound. Anything which illustrates a principle, even if it makes only one sound, is worth keeping. A list of instruments which are appropriate is given in Appendix 1.

Listening to children's music

Teachers need to consider their roles as listeners to children's music. The teacher might be quite unprepared for the child's music. It can be related only to what is already known and commented on only in the light of the teacher's own responses. The younger the child the more difficult this can be because s/he has absorbed or can express fewer of the structures that adults recognize and what is played can too easily be dismissed as shapeless. It may be experimental or improvisational, and it may change every time it is played, but this does not mean that there is no musical intention nor that there is no musical form. Teachers really cannot know how a young child interprets what is heard and played. What they can do is to listen carefully and to reflect back to the child what they hear themselves.

> A child plays an apparently amorphous piece on a drum. In it can be heard, at irregular intervals, a light beat followed by two strong beats. A teacher could say:
>   'There was a place where it went soft and then strong, like this.' (Plays.) 'I could copy it to make my own music.' (Plays as a repeated pattern.)

The response cannot avoid being within the teacher's own musical framework, but it can avoid being a restrictive re-direction of the music. The teacher finds something to talk about constructively and may suggest alternatives, but never says, 'That's not right. Do it this way.' If the teacher offers a model of listening and commenting in this way the children will inevitably follow suit with one another.

101

Listening to the music of others

> For most of us, there is only the unattended
> Moment, the moment in and out of time,
> The distraction fit, lost in a shaft of sunlight,
> The wild thyme unseen, or the winter lightning
> Or the waterfall, or music heard so deeply
> That it is not heard at all, but you are the music
> While the music lasts.
>
> (T.S. Eliot, 'The Dry Salvages', *The Four Quartets*)

Listening to recorded music with children can be a rewarding classroom activity if it is carefully prepared for and presented. The model of serious and careful listening that is already provided in the school is the essential first step. It is easy to forget how closely children observe adult behaviour, and if teachers are apt to chat to colleagues or parents while music is played the children cannot be expected to do differently. Even the youngest children, however, will form an attentive audience for music if they are used to listening to it at all times and in all forms with a respect that does not deny enjoyment.

Listening to music as a class activity needs planning. It needs the best sound equipment in the school and there should be no interruptions, which may mean aggressive notices on the classroom doors. The teacher should choose the best time for listening. First thing in the morning is an excellent time, but because of the demands of registration, assemblies and timetables, it is not easy to arrange to have it free. After break, better still after lunch, and the end of the day can be good, depending on the music and the mood of the children. A certain amount of ceremony helps. By making the occasion a special event one is able to encourage the children's best behaviour.

The classroom should have a library of CDs and tapes for the children's free use. The content can be regulated according to what has been done in the class. Music should be wide-ranging in style, reflecting different musical cultures, and it should include the children's own recordings.

CHOOSING MUSIC TO LISTEN TO

Music should be chosen in which the children can identify elements which are familiar or which relate to their other musical experience, while at the same time offering new ideas. This is partly a case of experimenting and building on success. It is not the case that the younger the children the simpler or shorter the music need be. If music is introduced in such a way as to entice the children to give it their attention they may surprise with the amount of time they are willing to give to it and the enthusiasm of their response. It is as well to be ready to introduce the music a little at a time, going no further each time than their interest holds and going onward in stages only as far as they remain keen. An open-ended, shared exploration of this nature is unpredictable but exciting. If it is made a regular, if not too frequent, classroom activity then the children will come to anticipate a listening session as eagerly as a favourite story.

Recorded music may be used initially to amplify a point made during group games, for example:

> The class listens to Paul Simon's 'Homeless' from the album *Graceland* following a discussion on the voice as an instrument and how effective it can be.

The teacher needs a repertoire of pieces which will appeal to the children and which can be used to illustrate, for example:

- unaccompanied voices;
- different ways to end a piece;
- two or three instruments entering a piece and falling silent at different times;
- changes in tempo, tone, volume and feeling.

LISTENING AND TALKING

Whatever the music chosen, it can stimulate discussion and may lead down unexpected paths. The teacher may have to abandon plans and try to find other pieces of music which seem more appropriate to follow on in the light of the children's queries and preferences.

These discussions provoke an enormous amount of exploratory language because the children are trying to describe not only specific points in the music but also their reactions to it. The teacher need do no more in the way of defining the experience for them beforehand than to explain why the piece has been chosen and what point there might be to listen for. This may be nothing more sophisticated than, 'You thought the last piece was too loud, so here's something quiet.'

The discussions about children's feelings can be difficult because the teacher will not want to label either the music or the feeling without due care. Yet it is far easier to engage in open-ended discussion of moods and feelings after listening to music than it is after reading a story. After a story the children's questions are always factual or they volunteer comparable experiences. But after listening to music their comments may be factual: 'What was that sound and how was it made?', 'Who made the music and is he dead?', or they volunteer comparisons between the music they have just heard and music they already know. Otherwise they begin what they have to say with, 'I felt like Christmas, like dancing, like laughing, like crying, like a circus ... I felt as if the piano was flying ...'

The complexity of children's questions can make it necessary for the teacher to make a score. This might be no more than pieces of coloured paper cut into various shapes and stuck on a large sheet to illustrate the movement or the main sections of a piece. The children can then follow the music as they hear it and point to the parts that they wish to discuss. The score may be re-made several times, each time in greater detail because the children are asking more specific questions as they come to know the piece. The children may be ready to write about the music (see Figure 8).

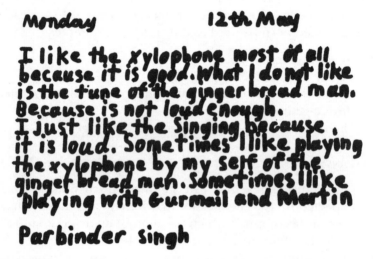

Monday   12th May

I like the xylophone most of all because it is good. What I do not like is the tune of the ginger bread man. Because is not loud enough.
I just like the Singing because it is loud. Sometimes I like playing the xylophone by my self of the ginger bread man. Sometimes I like playing with Gurmail and Martin

Parbinder Singh

Figure 8

CHAPTER 6
Music in the Classroom at Key Stage 2
Susan Young

The storyteller gathers the children around him without a word and, in the silence, rubs the stick slowly around the rim of the Chinese temple bowls, bringing from them a low, faint ringing sound and creating an atmosphere for listening, enticing the children to hear his tale. 'Magic bowls!' says one child with a loud authoritative voice, and the children ask him to make the sound again.

This chapter sets out to bridge the gap between the bland formality of schemes at work and the human hurly-burly which is the reality of school life. The aim is to show what classroom music for Key Stage 2 can look like in action by describing a picture of children making music and by detailing in practical terms the varied teaching demands implied by a broad curriculum. Threading through the chapter are some strong underlying ideas and assumptions about the nature of music education which shape these suggestions for the implementation of music at Key Stage 2.

Firstly, the notion of *children's music* asks teachers to recognize the intrinsic value of children's own work in music and to give it a credence which it still has generally not received. It requires teachers to hand over control to the children so that they all find music relevant, meaningful and fulfilling for themselves.

Secondly, it is not possible to separate the making and doing of music from the whole world of thinking, understanding and feeling that is the classroom. This is saying more than that music should integrate with the whole curriculum in the way that other subjects do, although this is important too. It is about the ethos of the classroom, that special togetherness and 'we-feeling' which teachers foster in their classrooms and which is very important as a source of reward in teaching Gibson (1989). This needs music for its contribution in generating and supporting those feelings and provides an environment, a sense of community, in which music can flourish. And it is something more subtle and demanding than simply saying that music *should be fun*.

Finally, it is proposed that skill and expertise are required for teaching music, but drawn chiefly from the very best of primary class teaching practice, and *not* just from the world of specialist music. Music asks the teacher to be sensitive, supportive and challenging and to approach

105

music teaching in all its forms with delight, enthusiasm and imagination. The expertise will be based on a knowledge of children's learning in music and a knowledge of *how music works* from which the teacher can draw a learning progression for children.

Above all, music is aural. Sound is its magic, and, as the storyteller opened the doors to a world of listening, so do teachers attune and refine their aural sensitivity and listen to the children and to their music.

Managing music in the classroom

Teachers should aim to make the class an environment for a full range of musical activities. To borrow the analogy of music with language once again, a comparison with the provision for language and for music in the classroom will highlight the ways in which the separation – isolation even – of music has profoundly affected ideas of what is appropriate provision for music in schools in terms of resources, time, space, grouping of children and class teacher attention. Strong messages about who music is for, how it is used, its relevance to our daily lives, and what forms of music receive most approbation are conveyed by the way in which music is catered for. The first major step in implementing classroom music is to re-think these practical issues boldly and radically, with an awareness of the assumptions which have shaped their organization in the past.

RESOURCES

The following is basic equipment for every classroom:

- tape-recorder listening set, preferably with junction box for several sets of headphones;
- library of tapes for listening;
- work cards for listening;
- song cards, song books;
- manuscript paper and other notation aids;
- visual scores, 'music on paper';
- blank 10- or 15-minute cassette tapes for each child;
- portable tape-recorder or extension lead for listening set;
- computer, CD Roms and other music software;
- books and wall charts 'about' music.

Instruments A glimpse in the music cupboards of some schools will reveal a sorry collection of instruments. These have often been selected on the basis of 'one each' for a whole class in the percussion band tradition. This leads to a large collection of inexpensive, small and ill-sounding instruments carelessly stored. A ruthless clear-out may be the first move and, for the future, a buying maxim of quality, not quantity. (A list of suitable instruments is given in Appendix 1.)

Ideally each classroom should have its own instrument resources, but more realistically a system of sharing decided upon by all staff can operate. Ease of access for all teachers and all children needs to be created with a centrally placed cupboard, portable boxes or mobile trolleys. One of the best systems may be to create several sets of music resources and rotate these around the classrooms each half-term. The advantage here is that better use is always made of resources which have a period of permanence in the classroom, while instruments left too long in one place can become neglected.

TIMINGS AND GROUPINGS

Different types of music activity demand different contexts, affecting groupings:

- whole school, several classes together – led by the teacher or other adult (for example, community singing);
- whole class sessions – led by the teacher (for example, games);
- larger group – led by the teacher, other adult or peripatetic teacher (for example, group violin lessons), sometimes led by a child (for example, a Year 6 child directing a group of Year 3 singers);
- small group – child-led (for example, three or four children composing together);
- partner work (for example, two children improvising a 'taking turns' song);
- individual (for example, at the listening set, listening to a tape and writing a review).

Music moments for the whole class slot well into those times of classroom life when everyone is drawn together to discuss and share: *the circle time* or *carpet time*. The activities for these times might be circle games, a song, or listening to either a live or recorded performance followed by discussion.

Extended periods of time will be devoted to music as a whole-class session. Examples might be: listening to excerpts of traditional and popular Indian music, discussing, making comparisons, looking at and learning about Indian instruments and then writing impressions in music diaries; listening to, and reviewing, individual compositions for blown instruments and discussing how they link with other examples of pipe music.

Group, partner and individual activities can integrate easily into the working day schedule. However, there is a temptation for the music task to be put lower on the list, the softer option towards the end of the day after the other, *real* work has been completed. It may also be used as a standby activity for those who finish other tasks quickly, resulting in some who never do any music, and a hidden message of curriculum priority. If music is valued and believed in, it must be given high-quality time in the daily schedule. Teacher time must be given to music tasks too, and they should not be considered the one 'they can get on with' while the teacher's time and attention are allocated elsewhere.

There are patches of time in the cracks of the school day – before school begins, at breaks and between taught sessions – which are often at present not made enough use of. Access to instruments and other equipment enables children to make full use of snatched moments. These can be organized with a system of requesting, signing up or an organized rota. Regular access to instruments for time to tinker releases the imagination and builds a bank of ideas.

The span of time and frequency for music learning tasks also needs to be considered if children are to make maximum gains. The acquisition of skills, aural and technical skills in particular, benefits from short, frequent doses and daily practising slots are best. It is not so difficult to build in some class aural singing games into the daily routine, or, for example, to practise co-ordinating two hands in echo rhythm patterns in the five minutes before children go to lunch. Individually, children may have periods of high motivation and intense activity when they wish to accomplish a new skill which has gripped their enthusiasm. Catering for the child who wants to do it again and again asks for flexibility on the part of the teacher.

Equally, creative work requires an adaptive approach to time. Some children who are methodical and painstaking may require long stretches of time to work on composing; others may work quickly and apparently spontaneously.

SOLVING PROBLEMS OF SPACE AND NOISE

Any discussion of space for music-making becomes entangled with the issue of noise, both between groups within the classroom and spilling out into other classrooms. Sound intruding into classrooms requires a level of acceptance and tolerance from other staff and the issue should be discussed among the whole staff before it becomes a source of tension. Lots of *musical* sound should be welcomed as a sign of increased musical activity, but children should learn to be aware of, and reduce, *noise* in any environment.

One tuned percussion instrument, with a pair of soft beaters (felt for xylophone, rubber for glockenspiel), or a guitar or zither, can be placed on the carpet or on a side-table. If one or two play or sing together quietly the sound can be unobtrusive and not disturbing to other activities. By having one instrument readily accessible there is an added bonus from giving the children frequent opportunities to play at snatched moments, enabling other children to share and pick up ideas. The instrument on the carpet can be exchanged for another every half-term or so.

Group and individual music-making which is more obtrusive in sound level will probably need to move to spaces adjoining the classroom. Ideally, such a space near the classroom can be set up as a *music bay*, a music workshop area, but all too often working spaces will have to be created from walk-in cupboards, corridors, cloakrooms, entrance hall and, in fine weather, out of doors. In these spaces there should be peace and quiet in which children can make music in the conditions which allow real *listening* to be possible. This solution may seem to be pushing music out of the classroom again, but these spaces can become an extension of the classroom. The *music area* becomes portable, equipment in boxes easily carried by the children, a piece of carpet and some cushions, a small table or clipboards for any notating, and a portable tape-recorder. Ultimately everyone must demand the workshop accommodation for music-making when new buildings are planned or existing accommodation is re-modelled.

Music lessons sometimes involve movement, dance or games which require a larger space and the allocation of some hall-time for class music sessions. This, of course, will need to be negotiated within the school timetable.

Within the classroom the noise issue is resolved when headphones are used for listening and for keyboards and computer composing. A music listening centre, with CDs and tapes, catalogue and written cards supporting visual material, will ideally be set up at a side-table. Headphones can help to integrate listening, playing and composing activities into the classroom. However, the effect of sound pressing into the ear is a very different one from listening to sound resonating in the space around and children should have a balance of the two.

The aural environment of schools is often very neglected in comparison with the visual environment. Music filling the classroom, or filling the school, can create or change the atmosphere. Valuing quiet times and spaces also adds quality.

Display plays a vital role in primary classrooms and music should be part of the display environment too, both for acknowledging children's work in music and for providing extra stimulus. *Aural display* provides a challenge, but performances of all types can be recorded and left on a cassette inviting people to play. Instruments can be put in a display, with labels and information written by the children.

Music on paper, in all its many forms and versions, can be shown as wall charts or in class books. Displays might located:

- as part of a wall display in corridor, hall or classroom;
- in the entrance hall where visitors wait, where parents come and children pass by;
- as part of a technology environment;
- in the waiting area for parents' evening;
- a special aural environment can be created in one part of the classroom.

Musical games and starters

A mainstay of the teacher's repertoire in initiating musical activity will be the games and starters that help to focus children's attention on a particular musical idea or opportunity. Games must have a clear music-learning purpose and can be used to initiate a sequence of work, to introduce a new idea, to spotlight one aspect or to practise a skill. The in-built organizational structure of games makes them ideal for whole-class sessions and the dynamics of playing engender a strong group feeling which in turn stimulates motivation and learning. The teacher must be sometimes the leader and controller, but is always a full participating member. Activities involving movement help children to internalize the sense of musical time structures in rhythm and form.

Perform a simple everyday movement, such as peeling a banana or stirring a drink, or draw a letter or number in the space around them. Think how the movement could be altered:

- slow motion or speeded up;
- the movement grows larger and larger or shrinks;
- the movement changes in quality, very heavy and tense or light;
- the movement starts and stops.

110

The activity can be extended by the children accompanying their own movements with vocal sounds. Link two or more movements this way:

Immediately after moving, play or sing the movement 'pieces'.

Purpose: To link the muscular sense with sound. To work with an idea and develop it, exploring possibilities and then combining ideas into simple structures.

Stand in two lines facing one another. One child moves down the pathway in his or her own way: galloping, skipping, jumping, but there has to be some regularity. The class must *find the clap* (or tap on their knees, which is quieter) which can accompany the mover down the line. The opposite partner follows and copies the movement exactly. The game continues with the second child showing a new movement.

With a partner, one child sets up a regular movement while the partner selects an instrument to accompany the pattern. Change places. Can the two ideas be combined in some way?

Purpose: To develop a strong sense of pulse, but allowing movement to set the tempo.

One child starts to tap his or her knees in a regular pulse. At a given signal, children tap their knees twice as fast, then back to tempo. At another signal children tap twice as slowly.

With older children, try three times as fast, three times as slow, four times, five times, etc.

Use a movement which is silent so that the underlying pulse is not heard but must be felt internally.

Children in groups of three or four make machines in which the parts move in different speeds relating to a basic pulse.

Purpose: To develop a sense of dividing the beat equally and of measuring the beat into longer durations.

All movement activities can be translated directly into a vocal or instrumental sound, and/or represented visually in graphic notation, or translated in rhythm time names.

Echo games sharpen listening by asking children to reproduce short musical ideas, to practise vocal or rhythmic movement skills, and to stimulate the children's imagination by demonstrating possibilities. While echo-clapping games are familiar to many, the basic idea has many variations. This activity can be teacher-led with the whole class.

Play an echo game using:

- 'nonsense syllable' sounds (zip, zap, ping-pong)
- short snatches of melody
- movements/gestures
- vocal sounds
- body percussion patterns
- combinations of these: for example, movements and vocal sounds

Try stepping the beat on the spot while listening and 'echoing' so that rhythms are sensed against a pulse.

Once the children have experience of these games in whole-class sessions the lead can be handed over to the children. They can play the games as a group or with a partner. 'Copying' with a partner can lead into the idea of 'not copying', replying with a new idea, or sometimes copying and sometimes not. This simple structure can be continued by two children with percussion instruments.

Spoken language is full of music: rhythm, timing, pitch, dynamics, accentuation. It is a good pliable material for games and starter activities.

Find rhymes, tongue twisters, riddles and limericks and build up a memorized repertoire, linking to language work.

Say 'Hello' and find the accented syllable. Say 'Hello' in turn to your neighbour around the circle. Can you change how you say it and add a gesture or facial expression? Greet your neighbour with an instrument. What kind of message are you giving? At any stage, other children can be asked to imitate exactly what they hear.

Purpose: To find imaginative ways to develop an idea. To find confidence in performing and a sense of communication. To reproduce sounds, stimulate acute listening to the original version.

Slide open vowel sounds from a high pitch to lower 'ooo ... aaa ...', with actions to help visualize.

Collect sound words: zoom, whoosh, boom, etc.

Encourage the children to stretch the words and slide the pitch, adding movements. Visual images – fairgrounds, fireworks or space – can help if needed.

The sound gestures/shapes can be fixed, combined, sequenced or linked in some way. Ask the children to draw the vocal shapes they have decided upon.
    Purpose: To encourage the children to use the voice freely. To develop awareness of pitch shape by using visualizing methods.

It is important in this kind of activity that the movement, drama and excitement do not detract from the quality of the sounds. The teacher's role is to focus children's listening attention on the vocal work by discussing with them and drawing them into a critical awareness.

Voices, singing and song-making

Children need activities which help them to use their voices with confidence in a range of ways. Both boys and girls should continue to extend their vocal experiences throughout Key Stage 2.

CHANTING AND RAPPING

Chant a rhyme and add one or two claps, gestures or vocal sounds at the end of each line or when it 'feels right'. Limericks work well.

On the spot, step rhythmically from foot to foot, then chant the rhyme. Change the tempo or dynamic: accelerate/decelerate, grow louder or quieter.

Find a rhythmic pattern to use as an ostinato (a simple phrase repeated throughout a song or piece as an accompaniment). A few words from the rhyme may make a suitable ostinato. It can be performed in movement, body percussion patterns or vocal sounds by one group of children while the rhyme is chanted over.

    Purpose: Most children will find it difficult initially to maintain a steady pulse while simultaneously chanting a rhyme. The stepping helps because the regularity is reinforced in walking. Changing the tempo may bring new difficulties of 'keeping in time'.

Teaching Music in the Primary School

Developing all these vocal activities can lead into rapping.

> Listen to raps for the way the voice is used, the main characteristics being changes of pitch and interesting accentuation.
>
> Use electronic keyboards to provide percussion backing.
>
> Suggest a theme for children to make up a rap: environmental issues, clothes, shoes or trainers.
>
> Rehearse the performance, which needs to be 'tidy and tight', and accompanied by appropriate movement.

Chanting lies on the divide between spoken language and song. Older children may like to think of examples of people using their voice in calls and chants: for religious purposes, to call attention, to sell newspapers, etc. This is one way in to speech becoming song.

IMPROVISING AND COMPOSING SONGS

Children at Key Stage 1 will have been encouraged to improvise spontaneous songs and this may be built on and developed as children come into Key Stage 2. To loosen any inhibitions about improvising vocally, a good way in is to improvise singing conversations. Usually the opportunity arises spontaneously in the classroom and, if initiated by the teacher with a sense of fun, most children respond and join in. Without earlier experiences Key Stage 2 children will probably need more prompting and structured guidance to encourage them to produce their songs.

> Starting points could be:
>
> A fairly short set of words, for example, about pets: ' I have a pet and his name is . . .' can become a song if the children are encouraged to 'say it till a song comes' (Davies, 1986). First songs may be fleeting so be ready to catch them on tape. Older children can work out songs more methodically, using a tape or an instrument to help sort, develop and fix their ideas as they turn words into song.
>
> In small groups of four, make a movement sequence for a singing game. This creates a framework for the children which supports and stimulates their song singing.
>
> Make songs for the infants to sing.
>
> Make up short jingles or street calls.
>
> Structures such as call-and-response forms can be introduced during

114

whole-class activity. An ostinato in movement, untuned percussion or on a xylophone at quite a modest pace provides a background for improvising and a sung call line on just two or three notes, for example: 'Today is Monday and what did you do?' The children improvise a reply about their 'daily routine'.

Use a simple sequence of chords on piano, keyboard, guitar or autoharp as a 'backing' from which melodies grow. The children 'humm' or 'laa' until ideas begin to flow, then try to crystallize their melodies. This is often best carried out as improvising which is tape-recorded and then ideas distilled from listening to the tape. Ideas or words often arrive with the melody. Chord sequences which can be used are:

- the reggae pattern: C major, D minor;
- the ubiquitous: C major, A minor, F major, G major, which all children know anyway.

Electronic keyboards are ideal for chord sequences and children soon find their own short sequences, such as A minor and E minor alternating. They should be encouraged not to change chord too quickly, but to be aware of waiting for one or two bars of the pre-set rhythm.

A rich diet of songs in the children's repertoire will enable them to absorb a fund of ideas for song-making and they will intuitively develop a sense of structure. The process of listening carefully to songs, describing and analysing their features, will 'make conscious' an awareness of these characteristics. This is a key element in appraising. Analysing songs may focus on:

- the sections which repeat, are similar, are different;
- phrasing lengths: two short phrases followed by a long one;
- the shape of the melody: rising/falling; any leaps or moving by step;
- structures: call and response; verse and chorus.

Using hand-signs, movements and visual scores are all ways of helping to reinforce the appraisal process.

SINGING

Describing ways into children's own song-making first in this section is intended to loosen the stranglehold of teacher-controlled and piano-accompanied class singing, which has been the dominant vehicle for primary music education for so long. Singing will still play an important part, but in *all* its diversity of forms. Using the voice is one of the most

115

vital forms of musical experience; it vibrates within us, is highly communicative and is usually the best medium for developing a sure sense of pitch.

There should be opportunities for children to sing:

- individually: either alone or with others;
- with a partner or a small group;
- as a class;
- as a school;
- with children of different ages: junior children singing songs to infants;
- with adults: with a teacher or parent;
- with larger community: festivals with other schools and parents.

A wide repertoire should be built up, including songs in a range of musical styles, and for many different contexts:

- improvised, spontaneous songs;
- children's own songs, sung by the composers or learned by the whole class;
- current standard children's songs;
- traditional folk songs;
- songs from other countries and cultures;
- community and religious songs;
- pop songs;
- classroom-owned songs;
- songs for occasions: the birthday song, the leavers' song;
- on-the-coach songs.

Children learn how to sing in stages. Many of the songs they ask to sing are beyond their present level, so they become accustomed to hearing a curious mixture of mis-pitching around them and a melody hidden somewhere in the middle. A core of songs with simple melodies, sung unaccompanied so that the melody is clear and at a pitch lower than that given in most song books, will allow them to increase their experience and control of vocal techniques. Children need frequent opportunities to practise pitching their voices, and the sorts of singing games which give children a chance to take short turns at singing alone, or in pairs, help them because they can hear themselves sing and then make adjustments.

Boys in particular seem to acquire a secure sense of pitch less easily than girls and lose their motivation for singing. Remedies are:

- careful training steps in early Key Stage 2 years;
- male role models: members of staff, parents, visitors;

- role models in older boys: some quiet praise to good older singers soon encourages them;
- attitudes and expectations on the part of all that they will be happy to take part.

If children arrive from Key Stage 1 having been taken through the first stages of learning to sing, early Key Stage 2 teachers can build on this. Otherwise it is worth working on some pitching games in the first term.

> Children sit in a ring and the child with the ball individually sings, 'Roll the ball, roll the ball, roll the ball to ...' to a simple melody of a falling two-note interval, just like, 'It's raining, it's pouring ...', simultaneously rolling the ball across the circle to the child. The activity can be varied by bouncing the ball. Two balls at once increases the excitement and a choice of when to sing: exactly together or one after the other in 'canon'.
>
> *Purpose:* To help individuals to secure voice-pitching using a limited set of notes.
>
> *Equipment:* a netball or tennis ball, depending on the age and ball skills of the children.

Children also need plenty of opportunity to try for themselves the range of expressive voice uses that colour the interpretation of a song. They can practise controlling dynamic levels, shaping phrases, finding different vocal timbres and making diction clear. They can decide how these are to be used in a particular song and make their own judgements about appropriate speed and character.

> Have a *clearing-up song.* When the teacher starts to sing or play it, it is a signal for clearing up. As the song gets faster and faster, so does the pace of tidying and putting away!

Instrumental work

The exploration of sounds and how they are produced and the making of musical instruments are activities on the fringes of music which have developed from work in Science and Technology. By shifting emphasis and allowing them to move in new directions, these activities can become musical as well as scientific and technological. This happens by listening sensitively and critically to the sounds produced and asking questions:

- How do we play and control the instrument to get just the sound we want?
- Can we make the same sound again?
- How does one sound compare with another?

and by beginning to structure the sounds into patterns so that they take on a musical meaning.

Children's improvising and composing takes different forms. Planning needs to take account of this and provide for two distinct kinds of composing opportunities:

- child-initiated composing;
- teacher-initiated composing.

These offer different scope for children's ideas and understanding.

CHILD-INITIATED COMPOSING

Child-initiated composing activities often arise spontaneously from individual instrumental exploration or from improvising in pairs or small groups. Musical patterns are found, or an idea comes for a piece, and children are ready to work on these and make a whole composition. Sometimes ideas are prompted by creative work in another medium, such as movement or language. Once children are used to composing they readily develop their own pathway as each successive piece suggests possibilities for the next. They should be encouraged to devise their own musical purposes in this way and to build a sense of themselves as composers, as they do as writers.

Suppose, for example, that three Year 4 children have opted to work with untuned percussion. The following shows how the children might progress and the ways in which the teacher can contribute. For the teacher to intervene in all these ways on any one occasion would overload the children and the strategies should be used selectively.

There are some points to emphasize in this model: the active role of the teacher in the process; the teacher is listening and asking if the children need some form of input, a skill or new idea in order to move the making on, or if it is time to pause, consolidate and develop the stage at which the children have arrived.

The process can be equally valuable for the children's learning if it arrives at any one of those stages; there is no necessity for every working session to arrive at a completed piece. Indeed, it may be a long time before children can arrive at anything which may be called 'a piece', but they will have been involved in important developmental stages in getting there, stages which cannot be rushed.

Children	Teacher
First session	*First session*
Children select instruments, explore sounds and playing actions and begin to select sounds and ideas they like.	The teacher reminds children to fetch and handle the instruments carefully. Once they have begun to work, she helps them to focus on the quality and type of sound produced. She provides some input on playing techniques.
They begin to be more aware of each others' ideas and start sharing, listening and talking about what they're doing.	The teacher helps children to be aware by focusing listening, drawing attention to the patterns being made, and asking others in the group to copy or describe them.
They look for ways to combine the ideas they have. Some fit together, others seem out of place. They have got stuck at this point and have spare ideas that don't fit.	The teacher reflects back to the children the strategies they have tried for combining ideas, for example playing the same thing at the same time, playing different things at the same time. The teacher asks questions to prompt divergent thinking and ways of moving on: 'Will you all play all of the time?', 'How else could an idea be shared by two of you, taking turns perhaps?'
Second session	*Second session*
Children play separately for a while, then together, remembering the ideas they found last time.	The teacher helps the children to review the work of the first session and the children decide how to move on. She listens without comment to the children's playing as they remember their work.
They sort, select and begin to fix their ideas. They make a recording of a rough version and some jottings on paper.	The teacher discusses with the children ways of finishing the piece. She asks them to think about how other composers have managed this in music they have heard.

They decide on a final form and practise it. The music is saved on tape.	The teacher focuses attention on the skills of playing in time. 'How do we do it?' 'Can you do it faster or slower?' She encourages the children to think about the quality of their recording.
Third session The music is practised and performed to the class.	*Third session* The teacher organizes an opportunity for the children to play to the class. She leads a class appraisal of the music and later reviews each child's part in the art work with the group who made it.

As children become more experienced their composing process may benefit from additional working strategies:

- notating: drafting and editing;
- tape-recording: listening and editing;
- reviewing with others: with peers, teacher, peripatetic instrument teacher, visiting artist.

Or they may benefit from fresh ideas from wider sources:

- knowledge of musical structures;
- listening to music composed by others;
- talking with a person with particular expertise.

Leigh and Alan reviewed their piece with the whole class. It was constructed from a series of melodic shapes, mostly scale-like patterns which were strung together but didn't seem to 'gel'. One member of the class suggested a rearrangement of the scale patterns. This was tried out while the whole class listened to and evaluated the result.

Children's music-making requires a listener. This is the teacher's most important role. The attention of a serious listener gives it value, reinforces the message that this is real music, accepted and acknowledged as being real and alive, and that it has the power to draw in others as responsive audiences. Modelling the role of good listener is vital. Modelling a listening response is the best way to encourage children's listening; haranguing them to listen both disturbs the aural effect of the music and usually has the opposite effect on the children's motivation to listen. So while the piece is playing, the teacher should:

- listen with concentration and without distraction;
- indicate interest and involvement by body language and facial expression;
- avoid interrupting the piece as far as possible;
- try to grasp the piece as a whole and analyse how it has been constructed;
- think carefully about what to say.

It is hard work in the classroom – in which a teacher's responses to sound are often dulled or tuned in only to certain types of unwelcome noise – to suddenly switch on the concentration needed to listen acutely, to remember the music and analyse it accurately. All too often, watching the children, observing their actions of playing or their behaviour as a group (and half an ear to what is going on elsewhere) takes the lion's share of listening attention. But gathering in the actual musical information informs responses to it, informs assessment of it, informs decisions in guiding the children's learning, and lies at the very heart of teaching. The moment the music finishes is the most vulnerable for the children's musical self-esteem and great care is needed to respond to children in a positive yet constructive way.

The teacher also has a role in *reflecting back* to the children aspects of their music. Input from the teacher must be matched with the children's intentions in the piece and their need for help as it arises. The focus may be different on different occasions. For example:

Focus on performing technique

- accomplishing a playing skill up and down all the notes on a xylophone;
- using the new notes and bowing learned in a violin lesson.

Input from the teacher may be to suggest ways to help technique:

- 'Blow more gently and the recorder will be in tune.'
- 'Try to change guitar chords more neatly.'

Focus on exploration of sounds and effects

- a piece which explores different sound qualities on the electronic keyboard;
- a piece which explores plucking sounds on a range of different instruments.

Input from the teacher may be:

121

- showing how to find a wider range of sounds by using different beaters;
- discussion about the quality of the vocal sounds.

Focus on composing techniques

- building a whole piece on a single musical motif;
- fitting parts for two melodic instruments together.

Input from the teacher may be:

- help with extending a section by repeating or altering an earlier idea;
- suggest trying alternative endings.

Children composing alongside each other build up a class musical culture as ideas are taken up in different forms, re-made and passed around. Children's compositions become part of the performance repertoire of the class. Learning to play 'class tunes' becomes a way of belonging.

Westlee is a special needs pupil in Year 6. For seven or eight weeks he would not touch the tuned percussion; although almost all the other children were playing freely at various times of the day, he shunned it. A tune made up by one pupil had become part of the classroom 'aural culture' and had been passed around; many pupils were motivated to learn the tune. Eventually, he felt safe enough to try it. He struggled with learning this tune for a day or two at frequent moments, the exact sequence of notes often eluding him, but there were many around to just help him when he asked. When it was finally perfect, he asked everyone to listen and, from this, derived a great sense of satisfaction. For the next week or two he still stuck with the same melody, but began to develop it, turning it upside down, playing it in turns with a friend, adding a drum beat to which he played simultaneously.

TEACHER-INITIATED COMPOSING

Child-initiated composing activities demonstrate to the teacher *where the children are* and indicate which paths to take next. The teacher plans composing tasks for the child designed to give the children opportunities to explore new musical ideas and techniques and, by presenting a variety of starting points, to broaden the range of their musical experiences. Children differ in the ways they think and learn, and teachers must cater for this diversity. While not attempting to be exhaustive, the following list suggests starting points for composing:

- sounds;
- instruments;
- musical structures;
- words;
- numbers;
- a mood;
- for a particular group;
- for an occasion, purpose or audience;
- for drama, stories, poems, dance, puppets.

Starting point: interlocking layers of ostinati

The whole class (Year 5 or Year 6), using hall time, listen to a WOMAD recording of Ghanaian kpanlogo music. The teacher models a listening response by attending with concentration to the music while moving gently in time as it plays. A second playing was preceded by a specific instruction, 'Listen to sound layers in the music and find a movement to match each new instrument as you hear it.' For consolidation the listening and moving were repeated several times. Sitting down to discuss, the teacher simply asked the children to describe what they had heard and listened carefully to their verbal interpretations for what these reveal of the children's understanding, repeating expressions occasionally and accepting them, never judging or rejecting comments. Building now on what they had described, the teacher offers a visual 'translation' of the music, drawing a pattern to represent repeating layers which inter-lock, using visualization as another aid to understanding. More information is given at this point and attention drawn to the irregularity of the rhythms.

Instructions are now given for a task to be carried out in groups of three or four during the remainder of the week in a music working space just outside the classroom. The children are asked to construct a piece using the same structure, playing four contrasting untuned percussion instruments. Giving clear instructions, the teacher is care-ful to use language in keeping with the children's verbal descriptions. Teacher-initiated tasks can sometimes flounder because the children misunderstand or are confused by instructions.

During the following days, groups work at the task. Some children have to be given more help to find independent playing patterns; it is easy to slip unawares into playing the same as your neighbour. Discussion focuses on how it feels to hear other patterns and to play one which is different. As work progresses a general problem arises as to how the pieces should come to an end. In a class discussion, a list of suggestions is compiled and pinned to the wall in the area where the children are composing.

The class gathers on the carpet to listen to the playing of a few of the groups. Instead of waiting for general comments, the teacher chooses on this occasion to focus listening on certain instruments before the pieces begin. 'Can you tap the rhythm of the claves when the music has finished?' 'Let's listen for how this piece ends.' And the teacher builds the children's skills of aural analysis. She listens intently and expresses interest and pleasure in all efforts, although for some there may not be very much to say: comments can do much to establish expectations, set challenges and make it clear sometimes that it is worth struggling for something even more rewarding.

Finally, coming full circle, the kpanlogo music is listened to again, with new insight and, perhaps, with true *appreciation*. The context of the music opens up a final discussion to promote multicultural awareness.

Notating and reading notation

During Key Stage 1, children will have been introduced to the first stages of representing music in symbols. During Key Stage 2, these early forms of simple signs and symbols will not be supplanted by others but broadened in response to children's needs, giving them access to a wider range of skills. As they progress through to Year 6 their skills of notating and reading from notation will be refined, the broad strokes of earlier years becoming a finer attention to, and understanding of, detail.

Although conventional notation is not stipulated by the National Curriculum, by Year 6 some who have had instrumental tuition will have acquired the ability to read notation proficiently. This can create a disparity amongst older KS2 children in this skill area, skewed in favour of the girls who tend to be in the majority of instrument learners. For reasons of equality of opportunity, staff notation might be introduced in the early years of KS2 to all children.

It is worth pausing to reflect on the issues of staff notation in the context of attitudes towards music. 'Being able to read the dots' represents a doorway to centuries of music preserved in manuscript. Other musical cultures have no such heritage, but are aural, of the present, carried in memories. Music of the classroom is mostly of this second type;

it belongs to the social group, is of the present and is mainly passed on aurally. Limiting this to what can be notated can be very damaging indeed and the idea that composition must be written down to be remembered is a complete fallacy. An over-reliance upon 'music on paper' can lead to a decline in other musical skills: aural skills, memory, spontaneity and improvisation. The KS2 teacher needs to be aware of imbalances in children's experiences: pupils who have instrumental lessons may well be heavily oriented towards written music and need to be encouraged to improvise, to memorize and to compose on their instruments in class; others will need help in developing staff notation as one of a palette of skills which can serve their own musical purposes.

It is important to have clearly in mind the value of using the many different forms of symbolization, including the two uses of a notation as a means for saving music and of giving access to music composed by others. Representation of musical sounds in objects drawn, written symbols, physical gestures and signals are all media through which the aural become visible, alternative dimensions through which it becomes some-how more tangible, communicable and workable. These learning *hooks* need to be employed by teachers so that children can form mental constructs of musical ideas. The only danger is that sometimes the learning medium can take over, and the senses through which they operate can become more dominant than the aural one; they should reflect always *back to the aural sense*, supporting, but not swamping it.

Different ways of visually representing music

- using objects to represent sounds: beads, blocks, shapes, multi-link, pegboard and elastic bands;
- physical gesture to match pitch, rhythm, tempo; conductor's gestures, action songs, hand-signs;
- numbers, letters written down; names of notes, rhythms written as numbers; numbered sections;
- shapes, patterns: drawn on paper; shaped by ropes on the floor; made by stepping patterns on the floor and movement in space; graphic scores;
- sol-fa pitch names and rhythm syllables: spoken then written; French time names (ta-te); African and Indian rhythm syllables;
- words: 'everyday' words and musical terms: 'faster', 'crunchily';
- staff notation: an early stage can be rhythm and pitch drawn separately, felt boards, five-line staff cards with counters for notes or metal sheet and magnets;

- staff notation: one staff, several staffs sounding simultaneously (left hand and right hand on piano music, or two recorders with different tunes);
- chord notation: letters and numbers, keyboard numbers and codes;
- instrumental fingerings: guitar windows, pictures of recorder fingerings, lute tablature.

There is a wide range of purposes for *music on paper* and these offer many different ways in which children can be introduced to staff notation. The following list tries to suggest some of these. It is not exhaustive, for the permutations of performing and notation could be endless.

Music on paper: purposes for 'writing'

Composing

- drawn or written by the children as part of the composing process: for example, a draft to help grasp the overall plan;
- for saving part or all of the piece;
- for someone else to perform from;
- as a framework for improvising;
- drawn or written by the teacher to clarify, explain or to offer new ideas.

Performing

- by singing or playing the pitch of a known tune (the rhythm information is not needed);
- for sight-reading a rhythm part;
- for sight-reading the pitch and rhythm of a melody;
- for improvising;
- for following a score when directing others;
- to help the process of practising or rehearsing.

Listening and appraising

- following a known tune as it is played or sung and identifying features;
- making a visual score while listening which graphically illustrates and clarifies how the music has been constructed;
- analysis and understanding of musical ideas helped and reinforced by reference to visual representation made by teacher or children or to a notated score.

Teachers who are concerned with children's written language use the term *environmental print* to refer to the written language which children will see in their daily lives inside and outside the school. *Environmental notation* is the musical equivalent.

Environmental notation

- notated copies of songs, children's music, pieces they perform on instruments; these should be openly accessible, like children's written books and stories;
- classroom display which includes notation: produced by both child and teacher;
- a full-scale orchestral score of music listened to; much can be deduced from the overall visual appearance – very dense, lots of black, or spaces and lines.

Staff notation skills for Years 3 and 4 This group activity should follow quite a lot of experience at listening and recognizing pitch variation. The work can be led by a class teacher, peripatetic teacher or other person who can read notation.

How do melodies move? Up/down, the same, higher/lower, by step/by leap?

Equipment: Cards with the five-line staff drawn on and lots of counters, buttons or any other form of notation-learning aid. A tuned percussion instrument to help pitching.

Activity: First the children sing a simple known song, or a melody they play on their instruments, and follow the melody on copies which give the staff notation without words. If the children are learning to sing with sol-fa, they sing the sol-fa and study the notation.

They are asked to write parts of the song with their counters on the board. Which part have they written? Can they sing it? Many children need time to 'get their eye in' and be able to perceive the five lines as one unit and discriminate visually between the four spaces and five lines. The expression 'with the line going through the middle of it' makes more sense to children than 'on the line'.

The activity can be developed by the children making their own patterns with five or so counters. They try to sing it first and discuss its shape: how does the melody move? Then it is played for them, and all look and listen.

> Give the children plenty of opportunity to 'write' their own music using felt-tipped pens and larger-scale manuscript paper. It is best to photocopy homemade sheets.

Organizing listening

It is worth reflecting on traditional ideas about listening to music. These are mostly a legacy from the 'appreciation' lessons of the past, and being clear about the values and purposes of listening to recorded music. The appreciating lesson implies a passive audience, but children need to engage with, and become involved with, the music. The teacher may provide for:

- moving to the music;
- singing or humming with it;
- drawing marks on paper, preparing a visual score;
- playing *with* the music;
- listening only, with concentration;
- following a score;
- listening followed by discussion, looking at outline scorings, recording impressions;
- listening with questions in mind, perhaps from a work-card.

These listening activities focus the children's listening attention and help them to gain insight into the music by harnessing other media. These are often linking the aural with other senses, which in turn heighten the children's response.

Movement, in the kinaesthetic sense, has a special part to play in stimulating concentrated listening and aural memory. Moving to music translates sound into time-and-space patterns, making visual and memorable the form of the piece.

Children need to listen to a rich diet of music if they are to build a store of remembered ideas for their own music-making. Listening to recorded music which relates to musical structures and characteristics which children have been working with reinforces a deeper understanding. Equally, listening to recorded music may be the 'starter' for introducing a new idea.

LISTENING TO THE MUSIC OF OTHERS

Listening to recorded music is usually organized as a whole-class session or with individuals/small groups on the listening sets. For a whole-class session great care should be taken that the listening occasion is a good one: that the children are receptive and ready to listen, that the sound quality of the equipment, CD and tape is high. The value of repeat listenings, the chance to be taken deeper into the music and make new discoveries, must be stressed.

Just as each classroom provides a reading library, so is there a listening library on cassette. Children find it difficult to cope with full-length cassette tapes and short, selected extracts of music on ten-minute tapes (five minutes per side) are very useful.* The classroom library will also have published tapes of stories with songs, and songbooks which have accompanying tapes. Recordings of children's own performances and compositions will be there too. Junior children often have music firmly categorized into 'classical' and 'pop'. Sidestepping these categories at first, by choosing music from other countries and early music, prevents the children's responses from falling into stereotypical ones, stimulating a fresh, more genuine response from them and giving something to build on in discussion. Also in these musics, the musical structures and characteristics are generally more clearly defined. A listening library might include:

- music for blown instruments: Peruvian panpipes, early brass music, music for recorders, Irish whistle;
- music for strings: 12-bar blues guitar, Hungarian gypsy music, Welsh harp, Indian sitar, reels;
- percussion: African drumming, Indian tabla drumming, gamelan music, jazz drumming (solo spots);
- songs: traditional British folk songs, accompanied and unaccompanied, men's voices and women's voices, reggae, calypso, rapping, South African choral singing.

Older juniors can keep listening records, similar to reading records, in which they note the music they have listened to and, perhaps, a short review of the piece. Writing impressions encourages the children to formulate a description and some evaluation of the music.

Talking with children about music

Most of what children need to know about music is learned through active experience. At the heart of this experience is listening, a rigorous, concentrated, sensitive listening. In much of this chapter descriptions are offered of ways in which the aural experience can be heightened and, at the same time, made more 'visible' or 'tangible' by employing what might be termed, somewhat grandly, *multi-sensorial strategies*. These strategies

* In order to comply with copyright legislation, recorded extracts should be short selections for study purposes only.

help children to disentangle and organize in a largely unconscious and intuitive way *how music works*. Talking about their musical experiences in all contexts brings this 'knowing' to a more conscious level of understanding.

But communicating with children about their musical activity is also couched in styles of interacting which take care of the relationships: the feelings which music learning is so bound up with. These feelings should be expressed by the teacher in sharing the child's response to music and ideas:

- being curious;
- being excited;
- being fully involved;
- taking pleasure and sharing the pleasure;
- empathizing and respecting individuality;
- looking after the children's musical self-esteem.

Using musical language Talking about music in all contexts will prompt the need for shared meaning, or naming, and will create opportunities for children to 'catch the language' of musical terms they are ready for. Engaging children in talking about their music, eavesdropping when they are working with others and listening carefully to what they say, reveals the children's own vocabulary which they find for their own purposes. For example, it is usual for children working just with untuned percussion to refer to a 'tune' when, in fact, they have only a rhythm. (African players talk of 'the melody of the drums'.) It is their understanding in context which is important at first. As the context widens, so the need comes for the use of terms with a wider field of common understanding and the teacher tunes into the children's vocabulary while, at the same time, developing and extending it. A frequent example of tuning into children's vocabulary arises in the situation of comparative questioning by the teacher about pitch. Younger junior children will hear the difference, but struggle to describe it with terms such as bigger and smaller, thinner and thicker, louder and softer, lighter and heavier. These all demonstrate an awareness of the difference and ability to discriminate: high and low are, after all, fairly arbitrary terms which have become fixed in the conventions of 'talking about music language'. As Wells (1986) suggests, teachers need to 'make a rich interpretation' of children's spoken ideas.

To help children 'catch' the conventions of music vocabulary, it is valuable to translate into words for children what is there in their own music, to *describe* in factual form, 'I hear a melody with five rising notes, over a single note which sounds all the time, "a drone" we would call it, and then I hear a rhythm pattern on the drum accompanying in the background.' If comments which give an indication of our own responses are added, such as 'I found the end especially exciting ...', we are giving children access to a 'talking-about-music' style which they will need if they are to become appraisers of their own music and the music of others.

During the time-span of music sounding, teachers and children should hope to be able to observe the no-talking rule. Talk, therefore, is confined to always the just-before or just-after moment. Listening may be 'open listening' where the aim is to come to the music freshly and openly and to find in it whatever the moment offers. Or it may be 'focused listening' when the teacher suggests, or teacher and child agree, 'What we are going to listen for.'

Types of talk   The types of talk will focus on different aspects of music-making. These may be roughly categorized as:

- Comments to develop skills, techniques (how to hold the beaters), how to sing better, how to listen well, where to stand when playing and so on. These will probably take the form of direct instruction.
- Talk aimed at focusing children's attention on parts of the music, the separate ideas which go to make up the whole. This might be very narrow questioning: 'Can you clap back the rhythm in the background?' 'Did you hear the strange tone of that instrument?' 'Did the music get louder or softer?' 'The tempo is very fast.'
- Talk seeking to develop their awareness of the piece of music as a whole structure: 'Laura starts playing and then who played that same tune later?' 'How was this piece of music put together?'
- Discussion with pupils for evaluating the musical activity and for setting it into the progression of work for that pupil: 'Good, you all listened to that very intently.' 'You are getting better at doing that.' 'Are you pleased with this piece?' 'Will you save it?' 'What sort of piece will you make next?'
- Sharing a personal response too: 'I really enjoyed listening to this piece.'

Group music tasks provide some of the best opportunities for genuinely collaborative tasks in which children must co-operate on the highest levels. Two or more children working together to make up music must translate their ideas into language in order to be able to collaborate successfully. This process of finding words to communicate their ideas successfully is extremely valuable in crystallizing their musical concepts. So too is the activity of teaching to others the music they have made up themselves. Often children want to be able to play music they have heard their peers playing, and the process of children teaching others their music is valuable for the same reasons. The melody made up by one child may become part of the classroom music, many others hearing it and wanting to discover how to play it, handed on one by one.

Planning

At the moment it would probably be true to say that planning for music is a somewhat haphazard affair in many schools, with the usual calendar of school events and, to a lesser extent, the needs of music for assemblies guiding the music curriculum. This 'serving the school' can also be said to extend to the situation of some teachers taking music-times with the whole school, or several classes, in order to provide non-contact time for other colleagues. Looking at the music-learning needs of the children shapes quite a different music curriculum.

First and foremost, planning for music rests upon providing resources, time and space for group and individual music activities, in the ways outlined earlier, so that it is there to be used by the children as part of the rota of integrated activities. Planning of musical activities should ensure that each child is involved in all of the processes within the spheres of performing, composing and listening and appraising. (For a detailed breakdown of these see Chapter 3.) Music activities should be recorded by the children and teacher using the system of recording children's accomplishments and activities during the week usual to that classroom.

Planning for music in a thematic topic has often been reduced to simply finding songs 'about' the subject matter of the topic. This may strengthen the children's interest in the topic, but it does little to contribute to the children's musical learning. Instead planning for music should focus on the elements and skills of music itself.

EXAMPLES OF TOPIC PLANNING

Focusing on the elements of music

Patterns: patterns in music, how they combine, overlap and interlock

Materials: sound qualities produced by materials, pieces for wooden instruments, metal instruments

Time: time in music and music of different times

Structures: structures, shapes and forms in music, sequencing, overlapping, interlocking, layering

Focusing on musical skills

Ourselves, listening carefully, using your hands and co-ordinating
our senses: the actions, moving to music

Focusing on the context of the music, time and place

An African Music and dance of an African country and its instru-
country: ments

Victorians: Victorian ballads, street cries

Integrating the arts

Light and   making up music for a shadow puppet theatre in the
dark: style of oriental theatres

Topics which focus on these genuine aspects of music can contribute to the children's real understanding of the subject. One with a humanities bias will concentrate on the music of other cultures, religions and times; another will take a more structural aspect of music: repetition, contrasts, shapes, patterns, layering; yet another may focus on the sound colours of music and how they are produced by instruments. Woven into all these aspects of music will be the technical skills of music: the skills of singing, of playing instruments, of listening carefully, of understanding and talking about music, of being able to use and read symbolic systems. A checklist of skills in a planning book is required. This list should be reviewed at regular intervals when devising schemes of work for a week, a term, a year.

The lead for a music project can be provided by a visiting musician, who may be a professional artist working with schools, a parent, a member of the music support team, a peripatetic teacher or another member of staff. It is wise to know what kind of contribution the visitor can give and to negotiate carefully so that the occasion is used to its best and can be built upon. It is vital that the teachers whose children are involved also take an active part in the occasion, both for its message to the children, and so that the work is closely understood and later followed up.

Another approach to planning is to highlight a week, fortnight or month as an *accentuated time* for music, when the classroom will be organized with music even more in mind, with the classroom lay-out altered to give special accommodation to instruments, displays and other equipment, which may be borrowed for the period. The music fortnight in the classroom can culminate in a 'show' for parents which demonstrates to all the diversity and depth of children's music in the school.

The role of the teacher

The practical advice offered in this chapter is based on the idea of the teacher as *responder, supporter and reflector*: listening, tuning in to children's music and making a careful response, and giving suggestions. The teacher shows and tells children what is there in their music-making and talks with them in order to extend ideas, to see new possibilities. The teacher gives the children a model for engaging with music: playing (in every sense of the word), singing, listening, moving and taking a delight in. On other occasions the teacher should be an *instructor*: giving information, offering advice, showing and demonstrating. The teacher should behave musically, without needing to be 'a musician'.

The teacher needs also to be a *manager*: organizing the time, space, people and the equipment of music to create access and availability to a wide range of music opportunities. Mingled in every aspect of these described roles is the teacher creating a positive 'ethos' both for and through music, in which the children feel encouraged and successful. Yet it is an ethos in which expectations are set up, effort and commitment are expected in the form of realistic challenges which are put before the children, and attitudes of striving towards quality are fostered. Assessment plays an essential part in the skill of challenging children. Teachers and children working together on music in an open way, listening and responding, can open the door to possibilities which might be otherwise unknown.

References

Davies, C. (1986) Say it till a song comes: reflections on songs invented by children 3–13. *British Journal of Music Education* 3(3), 279–93.
Gibson, R. (1989) Education of feeling. In P. Abbs (ed), *The Symbolic Order*. Lewes: Falmer Press.
Wells, C.G. (1986) *The Meaning Makers*. London: Heinemann.
WOMAD Records (undated) *The Talking Book*. Bristol: World of Music and Dance.

CHAPTER 7
Listening to and Assessing Children's Musical Composition
Joanna Glover

If the heart of music learning is music creation itself, then the heart of the assessment of music learning must be the assessment of musical creation itself.

(Loane, 1984, p. 227)

Understanding children's music: the listening teacher

As suggested in Chapter 1, the teacher may need to learn to listen in new ways in order to move nearer to the child's perspective. Understanding the children's music learning through listening to their work is the key to teaching that allows children to progress rapidly. The listening teacher will be gaining insight into the ways in which the child is:

- viewing the enterprise – how the child is thinking of the music, its purpose, the kind of music it is, how the music relates to earlier work by continuing or trying out new ground;
- responding to the sound palette available, the materials offered or chosen;
- ordering, structuring, evolving, transforming the musical ideas;
- drawing on experience, musical and otherwise for ideas and techniques.

The picture of the child's learning builds only over time, from lots of instances of music and in the whole context of the child's work in school. The following discussion outlines some procedures and contextual factors which appear to be fundamental and recurrent features of children's work. The broad categories used below have been chosen pragmatically as offering perspectives on children's work which may be useful in the ordinary classroom situation. The examples of children's music referred to are all of the 'child-initiated' kind; working times are given as an indication of various patterns of work chosen by the children. For an extensive study of developmental patterns shown in children's instrumental compositions within a framework of ten teacher-initiated tasks the reader is referred to Swanwick and Tillman (1986).

MUSIC MADE AS PLAYED

In an essay called 'Musica Practica' Barthes (1977, p. 149) writes:

> There are two musics (at least so I have always thought): the music one listens to, the music one plays. These two musics are two totally different arts ... The music one plays comes from an activity that is very little auditory, being above all manual (and thus in a way much more sensual).

There is something in this distinction that may be of the utmost importance in our understanding of the process that children go through when making their own instrumental music. A very important aspect of children's music-making is that of the way in which they engage with the tools of the job. For music made with instruments, of all the kinds that are extensions of body action we need to understand the way in which the playing activity is related to the stream of musical thought that emerges.

An instrument offers a visual lay-out of possibilities. Sometimes this relates systematically to the sounds produced – xylophone bars arranged in order of pitch, for example – sometimes not. Riaz made some music for tambour for which the plan was

'I play all round the drum once and then bang in the middle.'

(7 yrs, p.m., half an hour)

The musical result was a steady, controlled, soft patter, taking as long as it took to move round the edge of the drum-head, followed by a decisive loud and more resonant strike, once, to finish the piece. The appearance of the drum suggested this piece and Riaz had exploited the possibilities, using dynamics and an awareness of difference in timbre. Michael's tune is another example of a response to the visual lay-out of the instrument. Anyone who has lived with a Granton glockenspiel will have heard thousands of tunes like it, many of which have probably used B as the final note, the left-hand end of the instrument.

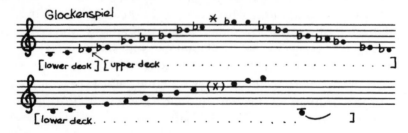

(6 yrs, 20 mins, music corner, alone)

Michael started with a left-to-right orientation, marking out by his playing the boundaries of the instrument, with a strong sense of rhythm.

136

He made a decisive ending suggested by the lay-out of the instrument. All this seemed to be conceived very much through manual activity.

The visual influence of an instrument on the player is one aspect only of the enormously complex relationship between action and sound in music that is made as played. For the inexperienced, action and sound are not entirely at the player's command as cause and effect. Coming to know what will happen if I *do* this, knowing what we will hear, is a matter of experience. The struggle to control the action that produces an imagined, desired sound is one that all performers engage in for the whole of their playing lives. Building a rich 'vocabulary' of sounds for use in imagination, knowing in one's head how they behave together, is one element of this learning. Physically controlling actions is another. Both are gathered only slowly and only through direct experience such as that of Riaz and Michael. Kemp (1990, p. 224) argues further that kinaesthesia through musical activities develops a form of musical 'knowing' which is based on the inter-relationships between muscular, perceptual and cognitive awareness and which is 'the essential ingredient of musically sensitive and imaginative behaviour':

> The central tenet here is that through whole-body experience we can know music and think music. The rationale is that the neuro-muscular sensations involved in the making of sounds, or responding gesturally to sounds, become fused with the actual memory traces or image of the sounds themselves. In this way recall of sounds and musical thinking processes are multi-dimensional, producing a powerful amalgam of sensory/perceptual *knowledge.*

Rosalyn and Chloe's music was made with a tambour with felt beater and a chain of very small Indian bells. Chloe rattled the bells all the way through, listening carefully to the soft jingling sound they made. As Rosalyn started playing on the tambour a pattern quickly emerged which she repeated over and over again. The pattern was made from two actions, a scrape and an accented strike:

'She did:
scrape   scrape   bang   scrape   scrape   bang   bang   bang.'

(5 yrs, p.m., time in twos, following whole-class session of 1 hour)

This can be analysed as being a rhythm pattern consisting of five crotchets, two quavers and a crotchet, grouped in alternating three and

four beat measures. For the children the music was *being* made, improvised, and was both thought and felt in actions. They were able to analyse
the pattern afterwards in terms of *actions* (see the verbal description
above) and see it as a pattern of timbres just as they might have learnt to
see *pink pink blue pink pink blue blue blue* as a pattern in threading beads: so
their music was a kind of *audible bead game* (see Chapter 8).

Patterning actions is one of the earliest forms of controlling musical
materials and we can recognize a stage in children's musical development when they become able to do this and another stage when
patterning the musical *sound* becomes predominant. A transfer begins to
take place from thinking in actions towards thinking in sounds, a process
which has to be fuelled by practical 'ears on' experience from which
mental sound imagery can be absorbed. Glynne-Jones (1974, p. 13)
makes a parallel point about young children's rhythmic patterning, such
as when marching and playing a drum at the same time, and relates it to a
Piagetian framework:

> We may be misled into thinking that children of this age who behave in this
> way, know exactly what they are doing and act with definite musical ideas in
> mind, i.e. to play intentionally a regular beat or time pattern, and to keep in
> time with each other. But at this time the intention is usually a general one
> and concerned with their actions. ...
>
> During this pre-operational stage of intellectual development, children
> need to explore and experiment with as wide a selection of musical materials
> as possible in order to build the foundations of ideas which later will become
> concrete, specific, and capable of analysis.

Often associated with action thinking in music is planning and describing
music by number. The first section of 'The Baby', a piece made by
Michelle with the help of Lisa, was arrived at and described in the
following way:

> After some time spent exploring a chordal dulcimer some music was evolved
> consisting of strumming groups of strings either up or down a certain number
> of times:
>
> 'I do this three times then I do that three times then I do this twice then I
> do that twice.'

Sometimes, as seemed the case here, the numbers are chosen simply as a
way of controlling the material, measuring in quantity, with the judgement of sound as very much a secondary consideration. Musically this

might seem primitive, yet the interface between number structures in the world and those in music is a complex one. Music's structural proportions and its measurement of time are always *mathematics made audible*. Children's grasp of number, shape and time emerges inseparably through their music and through other media. Feeling the alternation between the three groups and the two groups in the strumming became a significant part of doing this piece. (See Chapter 8 for further discussion of the links between music and mathematics.)

This piece, as it ended up, showed Michelle almost moving as she played across a compositional watershed frequently seen in the instrumental music of children of 6 to 8 years. This watershed is the moment when they suddenly recognize the potential for their music to be, as it were, object 'out there' with an identity of its own. This is the realization that the music can be made to be heard and made sense of by others, and that as composition it can be shaped and built. In this case, from the purely abstract pattern-making of the opening, an expressive idea suggested itself. The children made the first part, listened to their music and described it as 'gentle, soft'. Responding to this quality, a quality physically felt through the playing, Michelle added singing, making a three-phrase song following the pitches of single plucked strings and later the use of a shaker. Action and number planning pervaded the process but response to sound as sound came more to the fore as the work developed. Lisa's role as a partner player was to do as she was told. The two of them stayed with the music for several weeks, remembering it, playing it and not altering it beyond the version conceived on the first day.

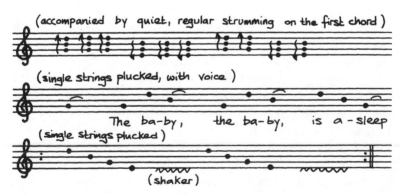

(Michelle, with Lisa, Year 3, p.m., 2 hours free choice)

The notion of the move from thought in action towards more abstract thought as being characteristic of progress is strongly rooted in our education system. We would be misguided, however, to understand

139

musical thinking in action as merely an early stage to be gone through and left behind as soon as possible. The physical actions of playing are an essential part of the stream of musical energy at all levels of musical expertise.

Voice music

A teacher of a Year 4 class describes the consequences of making an opportunity for some solo singing:

> 'Who'd like to sing a song for us?' I asked during a quiet moment. Not expecting much of a response I was amazed when James, a very 'bright' boy who has great difficulty in coping socially in class, or in any large group, burst into song. In a lovely choirboy tone he performed a song which we'd learnt in choir rehearsals. Judging by the colour of his cheeks this took a lot of courage, but for two minutes he held the class spellbound. ... Next I asked if anyone would like to make up a song; whereupon David, by far the 'poorest' boy in the class, started singing a song which he was making up as he went along. His song contained many elements of music-making which just 'happened' naturally and which would take years to teach. The song was shaped into phrases some of which were repeated; he used long and short notes; his words rhymed and were meaningful and the last line of the song had a strong feeling of finality about it. As a result of this his self-confidence and self-esteem have improved dramatically and he is much admired by his peers.

So often there has been an assumption that, when it comes to singing, everyone does it together. Consequently, despite singing being the one musical activity which almost all children do experience in school, teachers may be hard pressed to say much about individual children's vocal capabilities and may have had no opportunity at all to listen to children's songs, which offer possibly the most immediate form of access to their developing musical understanding. The easiest way to get a song is to ask for one. If the opportunity and support are given, even in a class situation, most children quickly lose any inhibitions they may have and will sing known songs or improvised songs and anything in between at the drop of a hat. For more sustained composing, voice pieces free many children to manage and work with their ideas in a more subtle and sophisticated way than does instrumental work, although there can sometimes be more difficulty in remembering exactly 'how it goes'; a tape-recorder can be helpful here.

Children's development in vocal music-making and instrumental music-making, although connected, take very different paths, particularly during the early years. The differences are significant enough to suggest that it is not useful to draw conclusions about children's musical capabilities and understanding on the basis of one aspect or the other alone. This is partly because of the obvious difference in the challenges posed by management of the instruments themselves, the voice being closer and more familiar than something which has to be blown, struck, plucked, scraped or shaken. But it has very much deeper roots in the different way that the two sorts of music draw on human behaviour. Vocal music is intimately related to all other uses of the human voice, to the whole gamut of expressive utterances, breathed, inflected and generally let loose. Most significantly, song is a form of language use and young children's vocal music draws extensively on their linguistic propensities and grasp of structure. In a parallel way, as seen above, *music made as played* is intimately bound up with body action. It taps a different source of natural behaviour, one more connected with patterns of movement in space. It would be quite wrong to suggest that the two are separate. There is obviously a two-way interchange between the vocal and the instrumental and indeed they are often conceived together. The idea of making an instrument 'speak' or 'sing' is a powerful one and likewise a song may arise from a dance or an instrumental action pattern. But in terms of children's music there are differences, particularly structural ones and particularly in the early stages that seem to be accounted for by the predominance of one or other sort of underlying behaviour. What is important is that teachers should give children opportunities and encouragement to compose and perform with the solo voice and then be able to respond to it.

Shabnam's song (below) arose spontaneously, although it was prefaced by 'I know a song . . .', a kind of conviction that the song was already there coming into her mind as she spoke. Yet it was certainly improvised as she went along and represents a common type of narrative song which children come out with in the same way that they make up stories.

The song illustrates the extent to which the child has already absorbed both linguistic and musical structures from her experience of song and story. She has a sense of the whole as in verses each with four phrases, a common pattern in children's songs and rhymes. The words are given rhythm patterns which fit them into this structure and which also on most occasions allow the natural word stresses to be mirrored in the music. The place where she 'goes off the end' of the musical line ('and she didn't know where it was') shows the story taking priority as she needs to fit all this in and come up with a final line which will close the piece definitively. The ends of phrases tend to fall and the ends of verses to be given longer notes with an emphatic way of singing to make clear the arrival point. The whole piece has a sense of shape and structure that

141

One day I was go-ing down the street, and I saw my friend and she saw a witch and I saw her too, and (swallow) we both ran to our house and our mother came with us and we saw that witch a-gain. So we ran back to our house and she didn't know where it was and she never went with, after us a-gain.

Some of the pitches were not very clear and these are notated with an X. (6 yrs, as long as it took to sing, end of an afternoon)

would be rare in a child's work on an instrument unless it were associated with song (see Johanna below).

There is plenty of research (Hargreaves, 1986, Chapters 3 and 4) to give grounds for thinking that this ability is intrinsically connected to a child's linguistic development. Children's spontaneous language development underlies teaching methods in language and literacy: fundamentals of oracy in the classroom, reading with meaningful material and emergent writing all derive from seeing the child as a spontaneous 'language user', rather than as an imitator of adult models. Similarly, in their spontaneous song-making children show an innate grasp of musical structure as well as their increasing experience of song models, from nursery rhymes onwards.

Extensive research in the field of children's song-making has been carried out by Davies (1986, 1992). Her findings have particular relevance for classroom practice because the songs studied were all produced within the school context as part of ongoing work with children. The approach to the children's music shows how much can be revealed if time and attention are given to both the music making process and appraisal of the resultant work. Davies's first study looked at examples of song-making by children across the nursery to junior age range, mainly 'in response to the invitation to "say it till a song comes"'. She suggests:

142

Progress in young children's composition can be recognized in many ways. It may simply show as greater confidence in handling musical materials; an increase in melodic range, melodies which begin to open out rather than remain closed round the same few notes; a developing sense of shape and balance of phrases, or a more sustained, longer invention. It may be apparent in a more apt setting of words, use of more varied rhythm patterns, including syncopation, and a more imaginative turn of phrase in the words themselves. Children can express appropriate characterization in their songs right from the beginning, helped in some cases by moving and miming to the words while composing. *As teachers, our role seems to be to encourage them to sing spontaneously, to show that we value and enjoy the results and to provide them with a developing musical vocabulary in the activities we introduce. Later we can share their dissatisfaction with too-easy solutions and help them to identify and discard trite phrases, pedestrian rhythms, too much repetition, poor shape, etc.*

(Davies, 1986, p. 288, my italics)

It is clear from the songs themselves that by the time they reach school the children *already have* a rich repertoire of musical song ideas on which to draw and that if the opportunity and encouragement are offered, they will readily make use of these and build on them. Davies's later work looks more closely at the musical structures used in the songs of 5- and 6-year-olds. Her study places importance on the structural aspect of music, on the grounds that 'the organization and relationships of musical events in time are fundamental to music's meaning'. The following observation is of the greatest importance for the way in which teachers listen to children's music of all kinds:

the role of structure in music is so important that we should expect it to play a crucial, leading part in the young child's development as a musical thinker. It is not so much that children are collecting materials which, once they have discovered the idea of form, will begin to be assembled into 'forms', but rather that, as the analogy with language suggests, the urge to make meaning in music (i.e. to experience satisfying musical wholes as images of time) drives the whole development.

(Davies, 1992, pp. 21–2)

Borrowing in music

Imitation is central to all learning. Much of children's learning begins with observation of the activity of those around them followed by efforts to re-create what they see. As a wellspring of creative activity, imitation is fundamental in nurturing the imagination. Paradoxically it is sometimes viewed with disdain, particularly in artistic activity where it may be seen as reflecting poverty of ideas and lack of originality. Yet in the process of imitation ideas are re-made, interpreted and perhaps transformed. The

143

process of reconstruction is a creative act in itself, allowing movement from the known to the unknown. Imitation is a major catalyst in children's compositional development and one that does not belong only to its early stages. It can have the function of allowing the child to move towards a new skill or approach, and of giving a sense of identification with the music made by others. It can also provide for consolidation, a resting time before searching for a new way of one's own. In terms of classroom provision it is of great importance that children are not asked to compose or to perform their own or other people's music in a vacuum.

Children borrow from their experience of music in many ways, imitating both musical behaviour – how people look and act when making music or when listening to another player – and musical material and structure. For the teacher, children's readiness and quickness to do this provide a key point of access to their understanding. They also allow for effective intervention, by teacher modelling of music-making processes and provision of a rich and varied range of musical encounters. Careful observation of which aspects of these 'models' children have perceived and chosen to re-create gives considerable insight into how they understand them.

Perhaps the most basic kind of imitative behaviour is copying what another performer does, imitating actions, perhaps complete with facial expressions. The feeling here is important: 'I'm playing the drums' seems to be 'I'm feeling how it feels to play the drums'. This should not be underrated as a means of getting inside the musical experience. It may be that there are clues to what music is and can do which can be gleaned only from adopting this first person perspective on what one has observed in others:

> Sharanjit modelled his use of a small pair of drums on tabla playing he had seen at the temple, using many different hand sounds and finger attacks and pressures. His music showed he'd absorbed much detail by watching and listening within a total musical experience.
> (8 yrs, improvised playing for the class, later with Paul, 8 yrs, playing autoharp, about 10 minutes each time)

Understanding Sharanjit's music depends on understanding the modelling process central to it and recognizing to what it refers.

Imitation can often be a starting point chosen by the children for making music.

> A song 'On the beach' arose because Sally and Michelle were 'pretending' to sing a song and accompany it on the guitar. Here, pretending to sing a song *is* singing a song and not only singing it but making it up, taking 'accompany-

ing' and 'lead' roles and using a repeating two-note tune pattern matched gradually to the guitar open strings, completing the whole with a standard 'fade-out' carefully graded down to nothing.

(8 yrs, several 20-minute sessions over two days, subject from TV programme seen that week)

Another recurrent form of borrowing is the unconscious imitation which draws on musical images that have been wholly absorbed and reappear when children make their own music. A piece by five Year 3 children was based entirely on reconstructing a simple sound image which had been used in a movement lesson contrasting movement and stillness. The opportunity for teacher input indicated by this is clearly enormous, particularly, it might be argued, in the context of movement response which, as seen above, gives rise to a particularly deep absorption of musical images.

A large category of 'borrowing' in children's work consists of their attempts to reconstruct music they already know. Particularly for very young children (but also for the inexperienced) the margin between 'making up' music and 'finding out' music that is already made is very faint.

Johanna reported that she had made a tune (6 yrs, 30 minute, alone but in a group of six). She played it in a very neat and controlled way, making an intriguing piece since it had such a clear four-square phrase structure. The other children instantly recognized this as 'Baa Baa Black Sheep', hearing the rhythm above the melody, which was Johanna's own, and bearing out perhaps the developmental priority of perceptions of rhythm over pitch (Moog, 1976). As with all children's performance, Johanna made the music her own both in its reconstruction and in the way she interpreted it. Her playing on this occasion pointed up how no two children's touch on a xylophone is the same – her light, quick actions giving clarity and a gentle but incisively rhythmic quality. Robert's glockenspiel tune also later turned out to be a borrowing, this time from the signature tune to a TV programme.

(Robert 8 yrs, over weeks, modifying, working alone)

Robert lived with this piece for over six weeks, building into it new thoughts as he went along and borrowing other material, particularly a two-stick idea following some work done with the class on beater techniques. Robert's way of working was to develop ideas as add-ons and modifications rather than taking new starts. This raises the question of how best to allow for a range of working methods, without always imposing either an 'improvement' request ('How could you make it better?' can be a most damning question if in the child's ears the music is complete) or very short, separate, time-limited, one-off tasks allowing no opportunity for the child to get to know his own work. The last recorded version of Robert's tune was as follows, to be viewed not as improvement or otherwise but as another way with it:

In a piece called 'Spanish Tap', Neil and Luke borrowed a 'tango' rhythm pattern which they thought of as 'Spanish'. They worked it out as a foot pattern first, a kind of tap dance, and then built their music by using the idea of exchanging instruments in turn, maintaining the basic rhythm and finally putting in a 'trip' pattern just before the end. The whole was viewed as a technical challenge and practised in great detail (Year 5, one-hour lunchtime followed by a series of practices). In this case the borrowed material is the mainstay of the piece and has a specific cultural reference.

Saiqua, Shazia and Nazia undertook to collect and tape-record some Urdu and Punjabi children's rhymes. The final tape collection was played with great excitement: would the listeners detect that one of the rhymes was newly composed by the group *in the style of* the originals? Their piece adopted not only rhythmic and rhyming qualities typical of the others but also a cumulative ending which exactly captured the sense of play and expected unexpectedness (Year 6, own time over several weeks). Here imitation took the form of learning to go on in the same way; the borrowing was of style and shape. Reproducing and getting inside known material was the stimulus for going on to create the new.

Several of the above examples illustrate the difficulties of drawing a line in children's work between the activities of composing and performing. Children's work demands flexibility not only in construing the roles within the making process of doing and giving to others to do but also in understanding the richness of the various permutations of the use of original and/or borrowed musical material and ideas. These pieces belong somewhere along a spectrum of composing – improvising –

performing but the fluidity of the processes has a richness of learning potential which it is important to preserve.

Music made alone

A further distinction usefully made when dealing with children's music is that there is music made alone and music made with others. These are also 'two musics' and both have vital but specific roles to play in children's musical development. Where music is a permeating part of daily classroom life, opportunities are available for work alone, in pairs, or in small or large groups. Some children prefer a particular grouping, for example, always alone or always with one other, whilst others will work in varied modes. Part of providing an environment conducive to creative activity must be to recognize this. There are both musical and social implications of different sizes of working groups which interact interestingly as one becomes the analogue of the other. What is certain is that, without some element of working both alone and with others, children miss out of certain aspects of musical experiences.

> 'To be lost in the work' is the ultimate state of mind I aim for when making art. ... To create an environment where 'to be lost in the work' is most likely to happen should, I believe, be the art teacher's concern.
>
> (Newick, 1984, p. 317)

Making music alone allows for total absorption in allowing one's own musical ideas to take shape. For the very young or the inexperienced two complementary modes seem to predominate. One of these is just playing or singing, free-wheeling almost. The other is finding an idea emerging and repeating it over and over again. In different ways both modes allow the player to absorb in a deep sense the cause and effect, physical and aesthetic, of what they are doing, and levels of concentration can be very high.

Harvinderjit (6 yrs) played a single pattern on the tambourine for minutes until the other children stopped her. She played with great rhythmic force, and was carried along by making this strong effect which gradually became too much for the listeners. Neil's (8 yrs) first work was on a chordal dulcimer, struck with felt beaters. He repeated a sophisticated, syncopated rhythm but free-wheeled around chord changes for 20 minutes without stopping. Such working alone affords the opportunity for getting control of material and tools but also of experiencing the power of the music as it takes one over. Musically these two exploratory modes are often found at the heart of composed pieces made alone.

147

They can also be a form of practising which contributes to the development of technical control in performance.

With greater experience children are able to manage and develop the structures of monodic music (a single line of melody), often going further in complexity than they might have managed within a group where many ideas can be in competition and it is less easy to take the time to develop something. Joseph, after some preliminary exploration, carefully built his xylophone piece from a melodic pattern which was repeated, moved up a fifth (a position chosen because it sounded 'the same') and then returned in a form shortened so as to make it end.

(Joseph, top infant, 20 minutes, alone among others)

Glynne-Jones (1974, p. 17) points out that this is one of the first 'intentional organizations' of pitch and suggests:

> The first intentional tunes made up by children often lose the verve and spontaneity characteristic of their earlier work; much more is involved in carrying out a definite idea in effort, concentration, memory and judgement.

As noted above, such pieces made on instruments are frequently less sophisticated than those made by singing.

Donna, with similarly little experience though considerably older, pursued the same strategy of sequencing a melodic idea, battling for a long time with the complexities of moving a pitch pattern involving chromatic ('black and white') notes up and down the glockenspiel. She had realized early on that there were more and less precise transpositions and that the precise ones did not always give a sound she liked. The final version balances an aspiring line with a downward sequence and the replacement of large leaps in the first half with smaller ones later on. The use of the repeated note idea was also calculated carefully, as were the pauses and a change of beater which was almost inaudible. The piece represented a period of learning about melodic construction that was a particularly individual matter. She wanted no help and no partnerships in the work.

148

(10 yrs, free time, lunchtimes, over a couple of weeks)

Music made with others

From the earliest age many children show enjoyment of making music together. This is an important musical force in itself and seems to happen in several ways.

There is music made together in the sense of children playing and making it up at the same time, as Ros and Chloe did. The children may be clear that they want to work with others but the approach is to carry on with their own ideas side by side rather than to be musically interactive. This is most likely to arise where children have not reached a stage where they are ready to 'decentre' and accommodate each other's musical ideas.

> Three 8-year-old boys made a piece of drumming music called 'The Three Beaters' which highlighted the emergence of this ability. The piece was made with the utmost co-operation socially and with considerable discussion about how the music would go, and who, in broad terms, would do what, when. The music was practised thoroughly.
>
> (8 yrs, one half morning)

In performance the rhythms were at no time 'matched'; they did not 'fit'. Arguably this lends the piece much of its impact, with which the boys were very satisfied. Listening to each strand in the texture it became clear that each boy had worked out and remembered a series of rhythmic ideas which were well played, showing control of rhythm, beat, dynamics and timbre. These ideas remained constant in each performance. The children were united in intention, in expressive aim. Musically, whilst they were ready to take cues from each other at strategic points within the large-scale structure of the piece, they were perhaps not ready to take on board and accommodate the rhythmic detail of what others were playing. Yet there is a need for some caution here. Systematically to construct the exciting, vibrant effect achieved by the combined drummings with the patterns overlapping, crossing and almost bouncing off each other would have taken analytical and compositional skills beyond the capability of much older children. To settle for combining patterns at a level which they could handle would have tamed the piece into something completely different. The children were collaborating musically on an expressive level and employing considerable personal skills to do so.

The notion of what it is to 'fit' musically is a huge and interesting issue far beyond the scope of this discussion. Yet it is often appealed to in the classroom context. Within some music it is clear what will count as 'fitting', in others less so. In working with children it is of crucial importance that the teacher invokes the idea of 'fitting' only in relation to musical structures which it is within the child's capability to grasp. In performance, for example, there is no point in expecting a child who has not yet internalized the feeling of the first beat of a bar or of the anticipation of a chord change in a certain progression, to *fit* with it.

With children's own compositions, the judgements may be harder still. Five Year 5 girls made a piece for wood sounds using three tuned and two untuned instruments. They worked independently but needed help in the final stages to sort out and fit together their five patterns, which worked as long as each begun at the right moment, a moment which was found and lost several times. Here the teacher's input was important in making sure the children both fulfilled their musical intention and understood the workings of it.

Working together opens up musical possibilities that are much harder for a child to manage alone. Christian and Scott constructed a tune which they wanted to be able to use in several different ways. Their music turned into a theme with two variations, the first of which was rhythmic, while the second involved the tune being used in a round. They knew they had to find a tune which would be harmonically satisfying, would 'fit', when played against itself in canon (9 yrs, one afternoon to construct, several more to practise). Moog (1976, p. 136) suggests that:

> The child is deaf to harmony at least up to the end of his sixth year, and probably for a long time after that.

This finding was based on the children's response to being played harmonic music in which parts had been altered so that they did not 'fit'.

> Not a single child showed the least sign of displeasure at the cacophonies in Test Series 5. They simply experienced this test as a sort of general sound.

Such a finding should not deter teachers from involving children from an early age in harmonic aspects of music, for example, accompanying a song with a drone, or using sticks two notes apart on a xylophone. However, using harmony in instrumental music is something which children will arrive at later than the use of rhythm and melody. Working in groups allows children to explore harmonic *fit*, and to learn how to use *dissonance* and *consonance* as forms of tension and resolution in their music. This is helped by listening to music which uses different harmonic 'languages'.

> In accompanying songs they have made up themselves children need not be limited to traditional harmony and can experiment with different chord constructions and progressions. When harmonic perception is beginning to develop, they need experience of singing with simple chordal accompaniment in both traditional and modern idiom ... and music played which employs a variety of harmonic styles.
>
> (Glynne-Jones, 1974, p. 86)

Interacting musically is fundamental to the processes of music-making. Some children are able to interact with others *musically* in ways they could not manage socially. Most exploit turn-taking, joining in, handing over and following on as part of their music. Neil and Luke (8 yrs) made a series of pieces in which they built up a repertoire of ways of exploring the musical relationships between two players. They used:

- echo and answering on drums across a space;
- playing together and then mirroring;
- playing identical music on identical instruments, keeping together;
- leading and accompanying, then swapping over.

Their work was characterized all through by an awareness of timing, listening to each other and playing with the music as it arose between the two of them.

When children make music for themselves they are, like anyone else, engaged in such activity, thinking aloud. They are involved in the process which is music: active, immediate thinking in sound, thinking musically. A child making music gives us a window onto his/her musical thinking and the understanding which underlies it. This thinking connects. It is part of the child's whole understanding of the world and response to it. It is caught up with the intricate network of capabilities the child has developed, perceptually, physically and interactively. The musical understanding which children's music displays belongs to the thinking world of the young child, that of a listening teacher to a very different world.

References

Barthes, R. (1977) Musica Practica. In *Image, Music, Text.* London: Fontana.
Davies, C. (1986) Say it till a song comes: Reflections on songs invented by children 3–13. *British Journal of Music Education* **3**(3), 279–93.

Davies, C. (1992) Listen to my song: a study of songs invented by children aged from 5 to 7. *British Journal of Music Education.*

Glynne-Jones, M. (1974) *Music: Schooling in the Middle Years.* London: Macmillan.

Hargreaves, D. (1986) *The Developmental Psychology of Music.* Cambridge: CUP.

Kemp, A. (1990) Kinaesthesia in music and its implications for developments in microtechnology. *British Journal of Music Education* **7**(3), 223–9.

Loane, B. (1984) Thinking about children's compositions. *British Journal of Music Education* **1**(3), 205–31.

Moog, H. (1976) *The Musical Experience of the Pre-school Child.* London: Schott.

Newick, S. (1984) Teacher/pupil relationship: 'Should the teacher stand so near, my love?' *Journal of Art and Design Education* **3**(3), 317–20.

Swanwick, K. and Tillman, J. (1986) The sequence of musical development: A study of children's compositions. *British Journal of Music Education* **3**(3), 305–39.

CHAPTER 8
Planning for Music in the Primary Curriculum
Joanna Glover and Stephen Ward

Music in the primary curriculum

At the time of appearance of the National Curriculum in 1987 (DES and Welsh Office, 1987) there was some consternation among primary school teachers that it was to be a subject-based curriculum with ten discrete elements along traditional secondary school lines. This contrasted with the primary curriculum as it had existed in many schools which had sought to provide an integrated curriculum through topic work and thematic approaches. Primary teachers' doubts about a discrete subject-based curriculum were founded upon the idea that knowledge is a 'seamless robe' and that the explicit distinctions between subjects are an abstract construct which is beyond children. The subject-based and timetabled secondary curriculum was seen as too mechanistic and unresponsive to children's *needs and interests*. Teachers, then, constructed a curriculum around topics which are of interest to the child and which allow different subjects to be explored in relation to the topic, rather than for the subjects themselves on a timetabled basis.

Although some high-quality and imaginative work was produced along these lines in some schools (Kerry and Eggleston, 1988; Ward, 1990), there had long been criticism of topic-based approaches for the lack of identification of specific learning targets, for the tendency to focus on a loose amalgam of humanities subjects (DES, 1978), and for the failure to ensure children's learning in a systematic range of subjects.

In fact, music generally fared badly within the integrated primary curriculum model on two counts. First, as shown in Chapter 2, it was often taught by *specialist teachers* who were not involved in class teachers' planning of the integrated theme and music tended to be artificially separated from the rest of the curriculum. Second, where there was an attempt to include music within a topic, this was often done on a tenuous and non-musical basis. In a topic on 'food', for example, young children might be encouraged to sing 'Food, glorious food' from Lionel Bart's *Oliver*. While the title and words of the song fit the topic, there are no *musical* connections at all. The links with the topic are spurious, and, further, the song may be a poor musical choice for a class who find difficulty with pitching the demanding interval leaps. The song should have been chosen to meet the needs of children's singing and wider musical development.

Another similar way in which music has been brought into topics has been to ask children to listen to music with an appropriate title, such as 'Winter'. It is questionable whether music can ever be *about* something in the way that such treatment implies. Alternatively, they are asked to compose music which *sounds like*, for example, 'the wind' in a topic on 'weather'. Here the difficulty is in moving beyond mere sound effects and into music. In both cases, it becomes easy to ignore the inherently *musical* aspects of music or composition. Listening to, or making, programmatic music which depicts something is a very limited function of music, and it might be argued that it has nothing to do with music at all. Also, composing programmatic music is hard to do well.

A new look at curriculum subjects

Despite the criticisms of thematic approaches to the curriculum and the introduction of the subject-based National Curriculum, primary teachers are still resistant to the idea of a rigidly timetabled separate subjects approach to curriculum planning and many schools seek to retain the possibility of integrating, and finding links between, subjects. Such an approach enables teachers to construct learning experiences for children which are inter-related, rather than a disconnected hour-by-hour move-ment through different curriculum content. It also enables teachers to generate a dynamic interest in a topic which relates to children's first-hand experiences, such as a visit to a castle in which children can explore the history of social life in the castle, technological aspects of design and building and investigate and listen to the music of the period.

The implementation of the National Curriculum has led teachers in schools to review their concepts of curriculum subjects and to discuss the nature of subjects. It has led to a revision of the primary curriculum away from the *integrated* model, where subjects are made invisible to children under the umbrella of a topic, and towards one in which separate subjects are explicit and recognized, but in which links between subjects are identified. Such a model is recommended in guidance for primary schools for the whole curriculum (SCAA, 1995). The advice to explore the links between subjects invites the teacher to make explicit the *nature* of subjects: what it means to know in science and how science is different from mathematics. So, rather than subjects being made invisible through their integration, children are instead encouraged to see the subjects as explicit and actively to find the *distinctions* between them, the *links*

154

between them and the ways in which they draw upon each other. Such an understanding of the curriculum, of course, requires that teachers themselves are clear about the nature of subjects: where the boundaries exist and what the potential is for making connections across the boundaries, so that the spurious connections engendered by some topic work can be replaced by real connections between subjects (Ward, 1996).

Epistemology, the study of the nature of knowledge, has a long and complex history. However, teachers should not feel excluded from a discussion of some of the principles of knowledge and it is possible to consider some basic examples to illustrate the idea. It might even be argued that teachers are especially equipped to deal with questions about the nature of knowledge because they are dealing with children's unfolding understanding of knowledge. For example, a philosopher would make an essential distinction between science and mathematics: science is essentially the systematic empirical study of the natural world – that which can be observed; mathematics is concerned with the logical principles which must be true in all possible worlds. So it is scientifically true that copper conducts electricity – we know by trying it out – and it is mathematically true that, in base 10, 1000×1000 is $1,000,000$ – we don't need a million plastic counters to try it out. Then, of course, scientists draw upon the findings of mathematicians in order to do their science when they make predictions about the thickness of a cable needed to carry a certain voltage. In their turn, technologists draw upon science to specify the wiring in a music sound system. An interesting point here for teachers is that children learn the logical principles of mathematics *through* the observable world of the scientist; for example, children learn the logic of numerical rules through counting actual objects – counters and cubes. So the teacher is frequently helping children to move between various aspects of knowledge in this way.

The exciting prospect for music in the primary curriculum is that, now that the planning teaching of music is coming under the aegis of the class teacher and is no longer the sole province of the school specialist, there is a real opportunity for music to be linked with other subjects and for its distinctive features as a subject to be explored. This leads to a consideration of what counts as music.

This is not the place for a treatise in the philosophy of aesthetics or a definition of 'music'. What is possible is to examine the nature of music as it is prescribed in the primary curriculum and to consider how it relates to other subjects: what are its possibilities for connections and what are the features of music which are distinct in themselves; what is learning in music and what is not musical learning. This brief tour round each of the other subjects is intended to play the dual role of helping us

155

to understand the nature of music itself and to provide some practical guidance on planning the curriculum. The links between music and each of the subjects will be taken in turn. The examples given are of children's learning activities which are given to illustrate the types of genuine links which are possible. The suggestions made are starting points and the ideas might be used at different levels with children of different ages.

Music and science (How music works)

The link here is sound itself. The science of sound concerns physical processes in which children learn about vibrations travelling through the air and to the ear and that pitch varies with the different frequencies of sound. For music, sounds are the raw materials; for science, sound is a form of energy for investigation and explanation. 'Getting interested in sound' is common to both music and science. Wanting to understand the behaviour of sound is common to both. The motives for doing either are different. In science the motive is wanting to know about sound as part of explaining how the world is. In music the motive is needing to know about sound in order to be able to manipulate it, to *do things with it* in an artistic context. Control of sound is needed in order to 'sculpt' with it, to use it expressively and to use it as a form of interaction.

EXAMPLES OF CHILDREN'S LEARNING ACTIVITIES FOR SCIENCE AND MUSIC

Sorting sounds
Put objects on a sound table and ask the children to sort them according to:

- how the sounds are produced: striking, plucking, shaking, scraping and blowing;
- the materials the sounds are made from: wood, skin, metal, glass, strings;
- according to the children's own classifications: e.g. fixed or variable pitch (one or more notes); those making more than one sound at a time; able to make a sustained sound.

Ask the children to make *sorted sounds* music to listen to or move to: e.g. wood on wood, skin on skin, plucked and scraped. Record on tape and appraise.

Controlling sounds
Set up an investigation into how sound is altered and controlled in

> different 'instruments': e.g. a single string on a sound box, a slide
> whistle, a set of chime bars.
>
> Let the children use the range of sounds discovered to make music
> which exploits variable musical elements which they have found
> such as the timbres, pitch, duration and volume.

In this activity the sounds themselves will suggest the musical structure to
the children. It is important that children are given the opportunity to
work the sounds into music in their own way. It is better at this point not
to suggest other ideas. The teacher should help the children to focus on
the musical use of sounds: 'make sounds into music.'

> A picture can be 'about' paint. Music can be 'about' sound. The materials of
> music are sounds and silences.
>
> (Paynter and Aston, 1970, p. 25)

Music is not an entirely abstract and aesthetic enterprise, but includes the
manipulation of physical materials and effecting processes in the natural
world. Making the links between music and science in this way informs
children of both disciplines: they learn about the physical processes of
sound in science and they learn how music 'works'.

Music and mathematics

> Number exists before objects which are described by number. The variety of
> sense objects merely recalls to the soul the notion of number.
>
> (Plotinus (AD 205–70); quoted in Stephens, 1986, p. 13)

The interface between maths and music is where abstract concepts, such
as number, become audible. If sounds are thought of as 'sense objects'
the patterns and structures of pure music are mathematical patterns
made audible. So, in working with sounds in music, in patterning and
ordering, children are engaging in mathematical processes, just as they
are when they work with beads, stones and other objects and their
relationships in the tactile world. So music-making might be seen as a
kind of *audible bead game*.

In the science activities described above, the children explore a
scientific concept and then move towards a music-making one. Exploit-
ing the links between mathematics and music activities engages children
in concepts which are, at the same moment, mathematical and musical.
The concepts are common to both. So the mathematics of music is not
just the application of mathematics, it *is* mathematics.

EXAMPLES OF CHILDREN'S LEARNING ACTIVITIES FOR MATHEMATICS AND MUSIC

Number   With very young children the *three-ness* of three can be explored in sound as well as with objects.

> Ask the children to make three-note tunes which are literally three sounds long; show the tune with three stones.
>
> Sing or play another short tune. How many sounds are in this tune? Sing it, clap it, think it, show it: one-to-one correspondence.

A beat is a unit of measure of time. The length of the unit is defined each time to give the speed of the music. It should be acknowledged, of course, that not all music is based upon beats.

> Children in pairs play a beat together. Concentrate on keeping together and feeling the regularity of the beat. Change to a new speed and repeat.
>
> Sing songs with a beat played as accompaniment, choosing songs of different speeds. Sing them without the accompaniment, feeling the beat inside.

Children can experience and grasp proportional measures such as 'twice as long, half as long'.

> Practise dividing the beat by twos and by threes. Make some music which is built by dividing beats in twos, or dividing beats in threes, or both; or by building on sounds which are *twice as long and half as long.*
>
> Use a number sequence such as 2:3:5 measured in beats as the basis for a piece of music (see Paynter and Aston, 1970, Project 23 for an extension of this activity).

Endless repetitions of, for example, a rhythm pattern are enjoyable, while the concept is absorbed, that is, *felt* as well as thought. This gives children the practice of repetition which is necessary to establishing their concepts of measure. *Staying with it* – continuing to practise until perfection comes – is an important part of musical performance.

Concepts of time are hard ones for children to build, but music offers the ideal vehicle for working with sequences and structures in time and *using* ideas of before, after, together, overlapping, longer and shorter than, of change and transformations.

Patterns   As patterning in number is included in algebra, musical structuring is patterning according to the different musical elements.

Make a pattern of two sorts of sound: scrape – scrape – bang; or wood – metal – wood.

Now make a pattern with two lengths of sound or two pitches.

Now make *music* using the patterns.

Show the patterns using multilink cubes (data handling).

Having made some patterns, use them in a piece of music which explores *transformations* of them. For example: rotation, reflection, symmetry.

Use computer software to make patterns and to edit and sequence them.

So while the science of music is concerned with music's physical part of the natural world, the *mathematics of music* is the way in which the player and the listener construct patterns using the logic of number systems.

Music, history and geography

Any music belongs to a people, a time and a place. Geography and history are linked for children in the otherness of the time and the otherness of the place. Through music, insights can be gained into other cultures. If pupils are to make sense of music historically and culturally, they should find out about the time, place and people to which it belongs. This is more important than pursuing a chronological sequence of 'musical periods'.

Children should encounter directly the music of other cultures and this should go beyond simply listening. They should be able to engage with it, perform it, analyse it and compose using features of it.

FINDING THE MUSIC

Over a period of time children should have a broad view of the music of different cultures. Children should have a genuine 'world view' of music

159

and not just see 'multicultural music' as the drum music of Africa or the Indonesian gamelan. Children should understand that there are different musical traditions within Europe, Africa and Asia. It is better, if possible, to find recordings of the real thing, or properly researched reconstructions and contemporary performances. The teacher should not guess what the music of Native North Americans was at the time of the European settlement of North America. If studying a place in detail, giving a narrow or stereotypical impression should be avoided. For example, 'African music' should not be portrayed by the music of a single region or group. Also there is more than one style of music in any culture. For example, the troubadours of twelfth-century Southern France had high-style and low-style forms. A little research goes a long way towards getting things into perspective. Children will be interested in the detail and the differences between different musics within a culture so it is worth aiming at 'getting it right'. Public libraries often have surprisingly good collections of recorded music from all over the world, as well as historical music.

CHOOSING THE MUSIC

In choosing the music it is worth thinking about the construction of the music itself. What aspects of it can the children relate to *musically*? For example:

- sorts of sound used: blow/pluck, skin/metal, long/short
- rhythmic patterns, quality of rhythm
- melodic patterns: range, shapes of line
- scales, modes, sets of notes used
- harmonic devices, e.g. drones, more than one part at a time
- form: repetition, call and response, dance forms

Any of these might become the focus for practical work as well as listening.

THINGS TO DO WITH THE MUSIC

Listen, then think and talk about the music   This can be done with the whole class or by pairs of children listening with headphones. The important thing is that children should be encouraged to *say what they hear*, describe the music *in musical terms* ('It has a tune that jumps about a lot'). The music should not be portrayed as exotic and strange. Children should be encouraged to find the links with their own music. In the first instance 'taste' – whether children 'like it' – is not so important, and it is probably better not to start by asking children whether they like it or not.

The teacher's role in this is helping children to listen by helping them to hear certain things and by showing an openness of response. So the teacher, who has children's respect in other ways, can lead children to an appreciation and awareness of music which is initially strange and remote. Finding the links *in the sound* is the way.

Use the music for movement work   Again, pick out the musical aspects and qualities of the piece and ask the children to respond with a movement sequence.

Make or reconstruct a dance to go with dance music: e.g. an eighteenth-century minuet or a traditional dance from Eastern Europe.

- Reconstruct some aspects of the music, improvising or composing (as a class or in groups). Don't pretend to reconstruct it all, take one musical idea to work from: e.g. the rhythm pattern.

Music in any culture sometimes has a particular purpose, such as a wedding march or a shepherd's use of musical calls to manage the flock. Children's composition can also arise from borrowing a musical purpose. This asks children to handle the musical elements in a particular way.

- Make a lullaby.
- Make music for walking into assembly.
- Make music for calling people to a celebration.

Perform music from specific times and places   The most obvious music which children can perform are songs. These often inform about time or place, giving verbal as well as musical insights into other experiences. Verbal and musical insights can be distinguished. In 'Rock a bye baby', the music fulfils the lullaby function whereas the words ('When the bough breaks') express the adult fears and insecurity of family life at the time. In very subtle ways music can take us beyond the verbal in our understanding of other experiences. Children should experience the musical sensations of another life. Singing a simple Gregorian chant, with its long-breathed lines, can help children to sense something of the lives of monks and nuns in the twelfth century.

161

SOUNDSCAPES

Any place or time has its own soundscape. Any location has a visual landscape: fields and trees, or sand dunes and wind towers. In a similar way there is an aural landscape which is made up of the kinds of sounds and music which are regular features of the environment: wind, traffic, playground voices might be part of the soundscape of the school environment on any day. The soundscape can be recorded on tape, listened to, discussed and reconstructed. When doing work on other places and times, children can create soundscapes. This can involve imaginative reconstructions when children make a journey through time and space and think about what the soundscape would have been like.

The musical point of this is the heightening of aural awareness and sensitivity to sound. The sounds themselves can be used as the raw material of musical composition and children can explore the links between these raw sounds the environment and the actual music of the culture. There are obvious programmatic features, such as those reflected in, say, George Gershwin's *An American in Paris*, but there are more directly musical features such as tempo, intervals in a melodic motif, which make the music work *as music.*

PEOPLE

People can often bring into school their own music of time and place. There are two dimensions here: people who bring the contemporary music of other places; people who bring the music of their own past. An elderly relative who has lived in the neighbourhood all her life might sing the songs and rhymes of childhood. The children may well find that they know the same songs. People from other countries might bring music from their culture. This may be very different, or again children may find similarities with music they know. For example, a teacher from Barbados sang songs learned in childhood to children in Bristol who immediately recognized the tune of one, although the words were different. Discussion followed about where the song might have originally come from.

Dancers can also bring a rich source of musical experience and participating in dance, as in music, can bring to life something from within the experience of another time or place.

So knowledge and experience of music from different times and places inform children about the culture of those times and places in an immediate and actual way, because music is an aspect of culture which can be reproduced anywhere at any time, giving the listener the experience of the original listener. At the same time they can give an understanding of the differences of times and cultures by experiencing the strangeness of a music which is remote from the current listener's normal listening repertoire. Through this the child learns about music that it is not a cultural universal, but a culturally relative phenomenon.

Music and art

There are long-standing assumptions about the links between music and the other arts, including visual art. Combined arts faculties in secondary schools have often been organizationally very successful and there has been a great deal of debate about the common ground between the arts and how they may be related within the curriculum (Abbs, 1987, 1989; Best, 1991; Ross, 1983; NCC, 1990). It is consequently often assumed that to bring, for example, art and music together is an easy and obvious teaching strategy.

A typical activity which might be given to children is to 'listen to music and paint a picture'. But we need to ask the same question we have asked about other activities: what *is* the connection between visual art and music and what are children doing when they try this? If the focus is on response, then the relationship is complex. The activity may be a good way of *listening to music* where painting is a way of tracing musical events visually. It may be that the music is being used as a stimulus to *making a painting*. The teacher should be clear about what the relationship is. It might be argued that attention to the visual and the aural are mutually disruptive processes and to ask children to engage in this kind of activity is to ask them to do something which is cognitively unrealistic. Quite often the child will make the link between music and the visual image by inventing a 'programme' or story about the music which is mediated through language: thus the child will interpret the music as 'sounding like the sea' and then represent 'the sea' in a picture. What is going on here may be only marginally musical. This point relates to the criticism earlier in this chapter of music for children being treated as purely programmatic. The idea that children can only engage with music if it represents things is false and limits children's musical experiences and interpretations.

It is important to recognize the enormous intellectual gap which the child has to cross in working in the medium of music and visual art. It is worth noting that the first National Curriculum Working Group for Art rejected the notion of a combined arts approach:

> The basic teaching of art has its own autonomy which has to be carefully safeguarded in any combination with other subjects. There are similarities in the arts which obscure fundamental differences. It is tempting to suppose that a common vocabulary exists in art and music because both use words such as 'tone, texture, form, scale, colour and rhythm', but the precise meanings used

163

in each subject underline how different each is. Each of the arts has its own mode of operation; the ability to compose a picture does not enhance the ability to compose a piece of music, or choreograph a dance.

(DES and Welsh Office, 1991c)

The first Music Working Group, in giving some brief notes about the ways in which music can contribute to other subjects, chose to ignore art altogether (DES and Welsh Office, 1991b, Chapter 12). Experiences with art and music can be planned alongside each other in a theme or topic. However, art and music do not 'touch each other' in the same ways that, say, mathematics and science do, as shown above. Fundamentally art and music are different forms of activity and response, arguably at opposite poles of aesthetic experience. They may be seen as two media through which to engage with a single idea and work in one may stimulate ideas for the other.

Carry out a colour-mixing activity different blues. Let this lead into paintings of different skies.

Carry out sound-mixing activities, trying combinations of different timbres. Make a 'patch' of music in which:

- three timbres blend;
- two timbres blend and one 'resists';
- all three remain distinct.

Make music which uses one or more of these 'patches' and is about blending the sounds themselves.

Discuss differences and similarities between mixing colours in paint and mixing timbres in sound. This can be extended to a discussion of the differences between the two media of art and music.

Music, language and literacy

The links between language and music are many and complex to the point where the relationship is of a different order from those subjects covered so far. Much of the music of the human race is vocal, and still more is probably vocal in its origins, and is inextricably linked with speech patterns and inflections. In looking at science it was shown that music flows from scientific activities about sound. Common structures are shared in music and mathematics. In the case of language and music there is overlap. Some aspects of language are musical and some aspects of music are linguistic. Music and language come together most easily in song. What are the links between music and language in song?

When a text is set to music there is an intricate relationship between the rhythmic and metrical pattern of words and music. Musical and linguistic patterns are intertwined. Children's early speech is 'musical' in its form and expression. Children's early language 'play' is musical with often rhythmical, sustained pitch and pointed repetition (Cazden, 1972). Children sing to each other, 'I know something you don't know.' As speech becomes more mature it becomes less 'tuned' and rhythmical as the purpose becomes more semantic. Classroom activities can develop this:

> Make lists of words that rhyme. Choose some of these and turn them into chants or songs, exploit the possibilities for different uses of the voice. Record these, listen to them and discuss the way the words and the music interact.
>
> Try the same activity using alliteration.

Children slip between speech and song in a very fluid way. In the classroom children should be able to move easily between the two. There are many ways of engaging children in these different forms. They need to explore the relationships between language and music for themselves. This is a part of learning to communicate and express things effectively. It is important that children become *aware* of the relationships between their speech and their music and that this is reflected in poetry and song.

One of the recent developments in children's language, and an important part of the National Curriculum for English, is children's *knowledge about language*. This was initiated on a popular level by the Kingman Inquiry (DES and Welsh Office, 1988) which proposed that, as well as becoming good language *users*, children should also have an understanding of the forms and structures of language: of how language works. This involves children in a reflective analysis of their own language, and the language of others. They should, then, understand about language variety: different languages, dialects and accents. In analysing different dialects and accents, they will listen to the stress and intonation used in speech.

> Children listen to a tape-recording of English spoken in a regional dialect which is strongly different from their own. For example, children from Southern England listen to Northern dialect. They note any vocabulary, grammatical structures, vowel and consonant uses which are different from their own:

> 'We wa' starving wi' cold, so we put us coats on.'
>
> In doing this they find that 'starving' means 'suffering with the cold' and 'us' is used as the possessive article, 'our'. They can also can recognize the musical elements in the language: where emphasis is placed, the length of the vowels, when the voice goes 'up and down'.

Recognizing the linguistic subtleties in a set text in a song will enhance the quality of the musical response. This will increase the children's sensitivity to both language and music.

THE NARRATIVE 'TEXT' OF MUSIC

Even before they begin school, children have a grasp of narrative form. Hardy (1977) describes narrative as a 'primary act of mind'. One aspect of this is children's sense of narrative *form*. They understand that a story has a beginning, a middle and an ending. Further they can grasp certain types of story-form, such as that in 'The Three Bears' or 'Three Billy Goats Gruff'. Lyons (1991) shows how the seven-year-old has a sufficient grasp of the structure of texts to be able to organize information in different forms, such as a letter or narrative story. In a similar way they can have an understanding of musical form: phrase structure, interval use, repetition, cadences, etc. There are links between musical form and narrative form. Both have opening themes, repetitions, endings. But these are expressed in different ways in language and music: 'once upon a time ...' as a beginning, or a crash on the cymbals as an ending.

Children can understand and use the structure of musical narrative in the way that they can understand and use story narrative. This is evident when children make up songs, because their songs have *form*. This form derives from their general ability to grasp and cope with structure. When composing instrumental music with no words music does not have to tell a story, like 'Peter and the Wolf'. Rather, it is that there will be *musical* structure which exists in its own right and which children can handle.

Music and movement

Parallel to music's relationship to language is its relationship to movement. Just as it was argued that the relationship of music with language is of a different order from that with other subjects, the same may be said of the relationship of movement and music. Together, language and movement might be seen as the two aspects of human behaviour in which music is most deeply rooted. Music and movement share the dimension

166

of time. Movement occupies physical space while music seems to occupy a kind of imaginary space in which, for example, melody 'moves' up and down, sounds grow and diminish, lines intertwine, textures become sparser or denser, and chords are built out of notes stacked up in a pile. The translation of movement quality to music or the quality of musical sound to movement seems so natural as to make the boundaries almost imperceptible. Movement in its rhythmic and dynamic life might even be thought of as a silent form of music.

For children the transitions between music and movement come as easily as those between music and language. Movement is a primary mode of response to music. Moog (1976, pp. 57–8) shows how repetitive movements are the

> earliest form of musical response to include something more than simple perception appearing from about six months as response both to the element of pure sound and to rhythmic pattern.

For young children the making of music is often accompanied by movement, or grows from it, as they dance while singing or playing an instrument. In the early stages, movement and action patterns may be at the heart of children's composing with instruments. To exploit the connection between music and movement is to capitalize on something that children already explore in their own ways and which helps them to understand each better. They can be helped to use movement as a way of grasping musical structures and expressiveness and also as a way of responding to them, and vice versa:

> If music lives within us and finds its energy, its dynamics, its shapes and patterns in the activity of our bodies, an activity which is itself a reflection of patterning in our thinking and feeling, so too it can come to be experienced and perhaps only truly understood through the same medium. For it is the dimension of time which makes music elusive and fleeting, yet time takes on a form of reality through bodily movement, we sense it through our muscular system, we see it visually in space, the progression of our bodies through space gives time an actuality. Through movement we can capture music and come to know its structure and its meaning by embodying it, by enacting it actually or by our imaging of physical movements.
>
> (Young, 1992, pp. 187–8)

In the Consultation Report for National Curriculum Music (NCC, 1992) the Key Stage 1 programme of study suggested that children should:

> respond to the musical elements, character and mood of a piece by means of movement and other forms of expression. (p. 25)

Some activities which highlight the relationship of music and movement are:

167

Movement and stillness

Move (by any means) and stop, holding a still position. Repeat several times. Feel the contrast between the movement and the stillness. Try varying the lengths of each. Take a new direction at each move. This can be done by the whole class in silence working in their own time.

In pairs, or as a class, match moving and stopping to playing and stopping on an instrument, one following the other, both ways round. Match the movement quality to the musical sound and vice versa.

Sequencing

Replace stopping with a different movement, a different musical idea. Feel the transition from one to the other and back.

Make a symmetrical shape, then an asymmetrical shape. Find a way of moving from one to the other and back again. Work a 'balance' shape into the sequence. Practise the sequence until it finds its own dynamic and flow.

With a partner, run your two sequences side by side. Work them into a new sequence for two. Take turns in the class to watch and 'listen' to these silent partner sequences. Think about the ways the two parts match, follow, oppose, interact. Listen to music that works like this.

Matching and interacting

Use three movement words, such as 'creep', 'pounce' and 'melt', to suggest a movement sequence. Practise the sequence and then match it with music which reflects the changes of quality, speed and dynamics. Or make a musical sequence of three sorts of sounds from the same instrument. Match it with movement.

Two together: find ways of crossing space, matching movements and keeping together. Then try one playing, one moving. Take turns to move and stop. Then alternate music with movement, then music with music. Listen to music in which two keep together or alternate or interact.

Moving with music

> Use free movement response as a form of 'active listening' to music. This needs to be built up on a basis of work which gives the children a vocabulary of movement to draw on.
>
> Use structured movement sequences, along the lines of traditional dance, as a form of listening 'analysis' to help children grasp the rhythmic and phrase structures of music. For example, in a circle, hands linked, step in time with singing a simple song. Make a pattern of stepping, changing direction at the end of each line. Let the children make a set sequence of movements, for example: '8 claps, 8 jumps, 16 skips anywhere you like', to fit with set music, such as an eightsome reel, as a way of grasping beat and structure.
>
> Use choreography of movement sequences for a chosen piece of music as a form of listening response and analysis together. Work on a sequence with the children over weeks through careful listening, trying out ideas and helping them to work out their own shape and structure for dance with music.

Conclusion

Exploring the relationships between music and other curriculum areas can lead to new understandings of the nature of music. If children are able to grasp these connections for themselves, it will give them more powerful ways of working with music. As we give children the opportunity to become composers and performers and to listen to and appraise music, we should help them towards an understanding of the nature of the medium in which they are working. As we wish children to have an understanding of the nature of language, so they should understand the nature of music.

> *Musicam nossi nihil aliud nisi cunctarum rerum ordinem scire.*
> (To understand music is nothing other than to have knowledge of the ordering of the universe.)
>
> (Thomas of York; quoted in Stephens, 1986, p. 14)

References

Abbs, P. (ed.) (1987) *Living Powers.* Lewes: Falmer Press.

Abbs, P. (ed.) (1989) *The Symbolic Order.* Lewes: Falmer Press.

Best, D. (1991) Art of the matter. *Times Educational Supplement,* 8 November.

Cazden, C. (1972) *Child Language and Education.* New York: Holt, Rinehart and Winston.

DES (1978) *Primary Education in England.* London: HMSO.

DES and Welsh Office (1987) *The National Curriculum 5–16: A Consultation Document.* London: DES and Welsh Office).

DES and Welsh Office (1988) *Report of the Committee of Inquiry into the Teaching of English.* The Kingman Report. London: HMSO.

DES and Welsh Office (1991a) *Music for Ages 5 to 14: Proposals of the Secretary of State for Education and Science and the Secretary of State for Wales.* London: DES and Welsh Office.

DES and Welsh Office (1991b) *Art for Ages 5 to 14, Working Group Report.* London: DES and Welsh Office.

Hardy, B. (1977) Narrative: a primary act of mind. In M. Meek, A. Warlow, G. Barton (eds), *The Cool Web.* London: Bodley Head.

Kerry, T. and Eggleston, J. (1988) *Topic Work in the Primary School.* London: Routledge.

Lyons, H. (1991) What Katy knows about language. In R. Carter (ed.) *Knowledge about Language and the Curriculum: the LINC Reader.* London: Hodder & Stoughton.

Moog, H. (1976) *The Musical Experience of the Pre-school Child.* London: Schott.

NCC (1990) *The Arts 5–16: The Arts in Schools Project Team: A Curriculum Framework.* Harlow: Oliver & Boyd.

NCC (1992) *National Curriculum Consultation Report: Music.* York: NCC.

Paynter, J. and Aston, P. (1970) *Sound and Silence: Classroom Projects in Creative Music.* Cambridge: CUP.

Ross, M. (ed.) (1983) *The Arts: A Way of Knowing.* Oxford: Pergamon.

School Curriculum and Assessment Authority (SCAA) (1995) *Planning the Curriculum at Key Stages 1 and 2.* London: SCAA.

Stephens, J. (1986) *Words and Music in the Middle Ages.* Cambridge: CUP.

Ward, S. (1990) The primary core curriculum in an integrated context. In D. Coulby and S. Ward (eds), *The Primary Core National Curriculum.* London: Cassell.

Ward, S. (1996) Thematic approaches to the core National Curriculum. In D. Coulby and S. Ward (eds), *The Primary Core National Curriculum: Policy into Practice,* 2nd edition. London: Cassell.

Young, S. (1992) Movement in a musical education. *British Journal of Music Education,* **9**(3), 187–94.

CHAPTER 9
Co-ordinating Music in the Primary School
Joanna Glover and Stephen Ward

Introduction

The case for the class teacher taking responsibility for the teaching of music in the classroom is made at the end of Chapter 1. Throughout the book it has been argued that the music curriculum should be about children's learning in all aspects of music, rather than merely their performance of songs, and that music should take its place alongside the other subjects in the curriculum to be taught *mainly* by class teachers. Since the implementation of the National Curriculum, progress has been made along these lines and it has been shown in Chapter 2 that primary class teachers are being successful in their teaching of the music National Curriculum, particularly where they are supported by a music co-ordinator (OFSTED, 1995). The *expert* specialist music teacher role is now changing in schools, alongside that of the subject leader who, as in other subjects, supports class teachers in their teaching of the music curriculum in the classroom. This chapter outlines the complementary roles of the subject leader or music co-ordinator and the class teacher: the skills and expertise which are required of the class teacher and the strategies which can be adopted by the co-ordinator to support teachers.

The music co-ordinator and the class teacher

As discussed in Chapter 2, there was a tradition in primary schools of a music specialist, usually someone who could play the piano, who would do all the music teaching, while the class teacher had little or no involvement. The exclusively specialist view of music education is taken by Plummeridge (1991, pp. 70–1), who argues that music should only be handled by the 'musicians':

> All music teaching calls for subtle and refined musical judgement ... it is wrong to assume that because generalists (in primary schools) can teach most curriculum subjects they can automatically teach music if they have guides and support materials. They may be able to 'cope' and *contribute* to children's musical education in this way ... but if music is to be a truly meaningful and dynamic part of children's education then the foundations of musical understanding must be firmly laid in the early years of schooling.

171

Plummeridge is right that teachers need more than 'guides and support materials'. Teachers need also to be sensitive to children's musical development and to what children are trying to achieve musically. But the point is that the music specialist is not the person to be able to do this with every child in the primary school, any more than the language co-ordinator can know about every child's reading and writing. It must be the class teacher who listens and responds to children's music-making and who can really help them on a day-to-day basis in the classroom. Implicit in Plummeridge's argument is the assumption that only special-ists have access to musical understanding. As argued in Chapter 1, almost all adults exercise musical understanding to a considerable degree, though not necessarily as instrumental performers. Since all children are to be engaged in developing such understanding from an early age, there can be no basis for seeing it as beyond the scope of any teacher to teach music, given that they have some training, as for other curriculum areas, in how to teach the subject. Plummeridge also underestimates the extent of class teachers' musical knowledge and skills.

Alexander *et al.* (1992) first drew attention to the need for increased specialist subject teaching in the primary curriculum. Especially at Key Stage 2 it has been pointed out that there is frequently a lack of subject expertise in many curriculum areas, notably mathematics, science and technology. In a way, the situation for music is reversed: primary schools have often had music specialist teachers with instrumental expertise. The direction which music now needs to take is to develop music teaching among all class teachers under the guidance of a subject leader. This co-ordinator has the role of keeping an overview of music teaching and learning throughout the school. As for any curriculum area this includes responsibility for curriculum monitoring and development, liaison with headteacher and governors, management of resources, and support of colleagues in teaching the subject. Other activities, however, may not fall within the role of the co-ordinator. If a school runs a number of extra-curricular music activities and there are expectations that there will be music for hymn practices, assemblies, concerts, plays or festival celebra-tions, these may or may not be the responsibility of the subject leader; indeed some may fall to a teacher with a particular instrumental skill. An ideal situation is that in which most, or all, of the staff contribute to these whole-school activities according to their strengths, and these may include those staff with particular instrumental skills. This is a healthier model for children since it demonstrates that music is something everybody can take part in and it allows music to become a positive force in the life of the school as a community.

However, the point is that the teacher with instrumental skills may, or may not, be the co-ordinator. It is shown here that the role of the co-ordinator is much more to do with general teaching and leadership skills than with some narrow instrumental expertise.

In their interim report the National Curriculum Music Working Group (DES and Welsh Office, 1991) suggested that music should become a part of the whole primary curriculum and should be taught by class teachers. This was made explicit in a statement on resources:

> While it is accepted that the bulk of the teaching at Key Stages 1 and 2 will be undertaken by general class teachers, ... there is a very small proportion of teachers in primary schools who have any qualifications in music, even at a comparatively modest level, and that many primary teachers feel ill-equipped and insecure at the prospect of having to deal with music in any way. The present 'escape route' of complete reliance on radio and television broadcasts will no longer be open to teachers attempting to cope with National Curriculum programmes of study ...
>
> (DES and Welsh Office, 1991, p. 67)

However, it is interesting to consider what the Working Group mean when they suggest that 'there is a very small proportion of teachers in primary schools who have any qualifications in music'. The statement implies that most teachers start from a position of complete lack of knowledge or experience. However, the authors' experience of working over the years with large cohorts of non-specialist students in initial training suggests that the majority of beginning teachers have instrumental experience which often includes having passed Associated Board grade examinations, have choral, orchestral or band experience, have learnt the recorder, can read music notation at a basic level, and/or have a range of other musical experience such as taking part in musical productions, dance, concert going or GCSE music. For example, in a cohort of 120 students on an undergraduate Qualified Teacher Status course, 75 per cent had received instrumental tuition and were able to read standard notation at a basic level. At the same time, most students claim initially to be 'non-musicians', 'unmusical' or 'no good at music'. They also tend not to expect that they will have to teach music, having experienced it as a specialist subject in their own music education. This suggests that co-ordinators need to investigate the reality of colleagues' experience fully and not take other teachers' instant self-assessments at face value.

Class teachers as music teachers

Primary teachers' uncertainties about teaching music are traditional and well documented (Wragg *et al.*, 1989). At this point it is necessary to reflect upon the relationship between the skills and knowledge which primary teachers hold, the curriculum which they teach and, indeed, upon the very nature of teaching and learning in creative subjects. The teacher's own skills and ideas may play a part but in the end learning, teaching must be a matter of facilitating the development of each child's own distinctive creative work. In doing so, skills of observation and judgement about which skills are needed next are of prime importance. These are teaching skills based on an artistic responsiveness which need not go beyond the 'ordinary'. Many primary teachers manage to teach art to children without ever being competent artists themselves. Similarly, they often encourage children to write fluent and imaginative fiction and poetry without ever themselves engaging in the writing of poetry or fictional prose. The reason for this is that primary teaching is not a matter of direct instruction or of simply demonstrating to children how to do things, but a complex interaction between initiation, advice, demonstration and response to the child's own efforts. Like art, musical education probably benefits most from a responsive observer and listener. Rowland (1984) uses the term 'interpretative teaching' to describe the process. The teacher is able to engage the children in musical experiences of listening, interpreting, appraising, composing and performing on the basis, above all, of his or her own listening and appraising skills, and possibly with the minimum of musical performing ability.

This model recognizes the skills of adults as *listeners* as of equal, if not more, strategic importance in primary teaching than the skills of adults as *performers*. It is in contrast with the 'expert' model of the traditional specialist music teacher where the performance skills of the teacher are displayed in the musical activity of leading the singing lesson to an extent where they replace those of the children. Such teaching can unwittingly replace opportunities for children to take a fully active musical part themselves in, for example, the performance and interpretation of the song; it can be that it is the children have the least of the musical experiences where the decisions about the singing – the tempo, the dynamics, the emphasis – rest entirely with the teacher, with the children simply doing as they are told. Just as children learn to write poetry by reading poetry and writing from their own experiences, they can learn to compose and perform music at the level required by listening and experimenting with their own music. In children's art, it is rare for the teacher to be seen demonstrating to children how they should paint a particular picture, although they will demonstrate some basic techniques of holding brushes and dealing with the materials. Music teaching, then, should be more about listening to and encouraging children's music, supplying basic techniques in support of children's own work, than it is about the teacher's ability to perform music or to compose.

So the skills which teachers need to teach children music are more to do with listening, interpreting and encouraging than they are of demonstration and telling. There is a need for some instruction, but these will be simple matters like counting in time, holding the glockenspiel beaters, giving ideas for recording composition in non-standard notation. As we shall see most teachers already have the aspects of musical capability which they need. What teachers do *not* need is to be able to engage in instrumental performance at a high level. In fact, it can be salutary to remember quite how narrow high-level instrumental skills are and how little the skills are transferable. For example, someone who has learned the violin to a high level of competence might be hard pressed to get a musical phrase out of a trumpet, and vice versa.

It might even be argued that a high level of performing skill by a musician or artist could impede the child's development if not held in check. Such a teacher might be inclined to intervene too strongly in children's own musical efforts. Just as a highly skilled artist might intimidate early artists by his or her skill as a demonstrator, so the skilled musical instrumentalist may overwhelm children's early efforts in composition and performance. As Rowland (1984) points out, the skill in teaching is knowing when to intervene and to move in with a little technique or strategy which the child needs at that point in his/her development. All teaching, especially of the young, requires encouraging the learner's stage of development and to recognize and acknowledge it. Of course, learners are always behind on expertise and the expert can always demean what they achieve. Good teaching is the skill of restraining the desire to impress with expert skill, but to recognize the quality of the learner's achievement *in its own terms*. Of course, in the arts, the learner's effort may well have real and unique qualities of its own which the expert teacher might never be able to reproduce, just as some children's naive art work can be unrepeatable by adults. However, even in empirical learning of, say, science, children's observations and understandings of the world have their own legitimacy. So *subject* expertise is not the only requirement for teaching. To understand this is to clear the way for being able to encourage any teacher to be able to teach music in the primary classroom. What primary school teachers do is to set up learning situations for children. This might include demonstration and direct instruction, but it also includes providing a learning environment with ideas and suggestions in which the child is able to engage in the activity of learning.

This is not a plea for ignorance. Of course, it is possible for skilled and knowledgeable musical instrumentalists to be good teachers. OFSTED (1995) found that, in the inspections of the early years of the music National Curriculum, the very best musical work was being done by the music co-ordinator who has some formal musical skills with his/her own class:

> The highest standards in the Attainment Targets are often found in lessons taught jointly by a music specialist and the class teacher, or when teachers who work for part of their time as music specialists are teaching their own class. (p. 18)

However, they also show that the class teachers without formal musical training did well in encouraging a high level of achievement by children in music. They go on to report that the traditional music 'specialists' were sometimes failing to meet the requirements of the National Curriculum because they were restricted to class and school singing lessons: where the teacher engaged in the musical activity and the children followed along in imitation. Of course, knowledge of music can make teachers into better teachers of music because a degree of knowledge and expertise is required in order to recognize what children are doing. The important thing is how that knowledge or expertise is used. In the past, it has been public performance by themselves followed by the children which has been required. Now the focus is on the musical learning of children.

Focusing on composition changes the picture. Whilst all music specialists have some level of performing skills, few have parallel experience as composers. This lack of experience of composition detracts from the understanding of the relationship of skills to musical creativity which is so central to a broadly based music curriculum. Composition becomes polarized between, on the one hand, what *the great composers* do – and therefore what we can never attempt – and, on the other hand, something unskilled and noisy that children *play at* in large groups and from which teachers expect much too little. OFSTED (1995) found that music specialists neglected composition in favour of singing and staff notation, and a lack of any development in children's composition:

> The compositions of pupils in Y5 or Y6 of average ability are often no more lengthy, complex, expressive or well judged, than in Y2. (p. 7)

The respect which has grown for children's art work at its best is still missing from children's music composition. While teachers can recognize good art work by children, they are unsure how children's music sounds. Even music specialists are frequently unaware of the skills needed in composition and how to develop them.

The argument then is, first that non-specialist teachers can teach music, and second that the specialist needs to refrain from the tendency to perform and, instead, to listen to the children's performance and composition. It may be that the specialist has to *pretend*, and certainly to step back into a listening mode. Specialists also needs to be removed from the context of demonstrating their own performance as a way of legitimating themselves in the school.

What is needed is enthusiasm and wonder at what children can do and an understanding of children's musical development. This is not to say that there are no skills required. What the teacher needs to do to support the child in composition does not require instrumental expertise, but it does require skills of teaching and expertise in children's learning.

In the arts, the beauty of teaching is being able to say to children, 'You did it, I could never have done it like that.' In any creative field, within and beyond the arts, an individual's skills need to be matched with the scope to exercise creative decision-making according to a personal 'vision'. Children have to learn to develop their own inner creative sense, just as they have to learn skills and knowledge. This development takes place alongside the acquisition of skills and is intrinsically connected to it. Teachers need to provide genuinely creative opportunities in which children can devise and act on their individual creative ideas. In music this can be within composition or performance or in creative responses as listeners through words, dance or other media. The quality of teaching interaction through which teachers help children to clarify and follow through their creative ideas is crucial to the quality of work produced. Children then take control of their own learning and development, but they can't do it all themselves. This is not to say that in arts education *anything goes*. However, to be able to initiate, encourage and respond to children's music, teachers do not require a high level of technical instrumental skill or musical literacy.

The aim for the development of music with class teachers is to foster their confidence and help them to utilize the skills, knowledge and experience which they already possess:

> Primary teachers often have low self-esteem as musicians, and insufficient access to in-service training which will help them to use their abilities constructively.

> (OFSTED, 1995, p. 4)

As OFSTED found (Mills, 1994), class teachers under-rate themselves:

> It was not unusual for class teachers to explain to HMI that they were 'not musical' and very worried about teaching music, and then teach a lesson which led pupils to make good progress as composers, performers or

appraisers of music. Class teachers who under-rated their music teaching were often found particularly in schools which had recently lost a teacher with specialist qualifications in music. What the successful class teachers brought to their music lessons was their ability to observe pupils, work out what they could do, and plan an activity which would move them forward. Many of them also understood that music lessons exist so that pupils, rather than teachers, can do musical activities, and planned lessons which did not make unreasonable demands of themselves as musicians. (p. 193)

Campbell (1985) finds that curriculum co-ordinators are often ineffective because of the power relationships in schools; they need to be collegial and find it difficult to direct other teachers. Other teachers pretend to take advice, but don't alter their practice. Galton (1996) also argues that curriculum co-ordinators are ineffective more because they lack any theoretical model of how teachers learn to teach and how skills in teaching develop. Another problem for co-ordinators is their inexperience of teaching other adults and the lack of expectation of training others in the teaching profession. While primary teachers are avid teachers of children, they are very often reticent about developing learning in other adults.

These point to the need for more direct intervention by subject leaders. The implication is that teachers will be threatened by direct intervention. However, in the case of music, many teachers need to be helped to understand that they can do anything at all. Galton's position is that teachers wish to protect their professional knowledge and not be threatened by advice. In music, they just want to hand it all over. So a different set of skills is needed which relates to getting people started.

In some ways the music co-ordinator has the hardest job of all. S/he has enticed teachers into their role as music teachers and must convince them that they have, or can easily acquire, the skills needed.

Skills for teaching music

A major part of the music co-ordinator's role, then, is to enable teachers to realize their musical capabilities and to use them in the classroom. Chapter 1 identified a list of abilities needed by any teacher, specialist or not, in handling music in the classroom. These combined ordinary adult musical abilities with a range of teaching skills, most of which are transferable across the curriculum. From the perspective of the co-ordinator, these are the skills which are being looked for as each teacher develops work in music with their own class. In schools where some staff lack initial training in music teaching, or are unused to doing it themselves, the co-ordinator may have to clarify approaches based on these skills and perhaps help colleagues to develop them. The following sections outline each skill in turn, particularly identifying ways in which their development might be facilitated.

BEING A CAREFUL LISTENER

The teacher needs to be a demonstrably careful and perceptive listener to children's work and to other music. This entails a range of skills of listening and aural analysis:

- giving attention to music and responding to it as a whole;
- noticing the detail of how music is constructed, how the musical elements are used separately contributing to the whole effect;
- noticing details of performance, quality of sound, interpretation, projection and communication of the spirit of the music;
- bringing an understanding of the context and function of the music to bear on how it is heard;
- being able to enter into the musical moment with empathy.

It also entails being able to model attentive and responsive listening so that children learn by seeing what it is to be involved in music as a listener. When the music is the children's own, they benefit immeasurably from the sense that a listener is giving their music this quality of undivided attention and is taking it seriously. This kind of listening is fundamental in making the ongoing assessment of *how the music sounds* which is essential to any teaching in music. Not only is it central in teaching children to listen in similar ways when they are in the audience role; such listening also underpins all practical work in music, whether singing, playing, or as part of the composing process. Teachers and children alike must be able to listen perceptively and use what this tells them in moving their work forward.

Teachers may need reassurance that children's work will sound different from adult's music and that it will take some time to become familiar with what to expect. They may simply need encouragement to realize how important just listening can be and to feel confident in their abilities to notice musical detail and trust their ears.

USING MUSICAL LANGUAGE

The teacher needs to be able to use language confidently in a musical context:

- to use musical terms to describe music listened to, such as: melody, rhythm, phrase;
- to appraise music in the wider sense;
- to give feedback on children's work, to reflect back to children what the teacher hears;
- to help children distinguish between different sorts of musical talk (see Chapter 3).

Schools as a whole need to identify a musical vocabulary in which consistently to discuss music composed, performed and listened to. Teachers need to be confident with this vocabulary which does not have to be extensively technical but should incorporate the basic sets of musical terms. Similarly, there can be agreement to introduce children to different ways of talking about music. Examples are: describing the music itself; talking about its background, purposes and context; describing personal responses to music; making judgements of taste and value.

Teachers may need practical or listening experiences, as within a staff meeting or staff development session, to give a context for talking about music and checking vocabulary. Or the co-ordinator might talk to colleagues about examples of children's work, giving indications of what to listen for and modelling the different kinds of talk and vocabulary that might be used with a class. Mostly it is not so much that the vocabulary is unfamiliar as that reassurance or clarification is needed about its precise application.

TAKING AN OPEN APPROACH TO MUSIC

The teacher needs to have an imaginative approach to, and evident enthusiasm for, as wide a variety of music as possible, including children's own work. This is hard to legislate for, though it draws on the ways in which many people respond to music in their own lives. As an attitude to be cultivated, it is based on a willingness to be open to a range of music as a listener and to persevere in becoming familiar with new music until interest and, ideally, enjoyment comes of its own accord. Irrespective of personal taste, taking an imaginative approach to music is no different from such an approach in any curriculum area. It involves taking a questioning approach, looking for different ways of engaging with music, looking out for varied opportunities to find new musical starting points (people, instruments, video/audio recordings, visits) and working from these, involving the children in the process.

It may help to have conversations among colleagues about each person's own musical tastes and interests and to try to dispel the idea that anyone is expected to know everything about any music which is brought into the classroom. It is understood that teachers will all have different tastes and experience, as will the children. The question can then be raised as to how children can be encouraged to be open to a wide range of music.

INVESTIGATING MUSIC WITH INTEREST

Teachers need to be able to teach children investigative skills so that they can learn to ask questions and find out about music that they hear. These are mainly skills which are transferable across the curriculum. They include asking questions, such as about how music was composed, who by, under what circumstances, and for what, what decisions a performer has had to make, and what difficulties have been faced in performing the music. Sources of information will include interviewing people, using books, scores (not necessarily in a technical way), paintings and photographs, videos and CD-ROMs. More directly, investigating music includes listening over and over again and discovering in more detail how the music 'goes'.

Teachers will probably need very little help with this aspect once it has been introduced as an approach to be valued in a musical context. It breaks down the idea that extensive musical knowledge is necessarily required in advance of introducing a topic with children. Using approaches familiar in history can be very useful here; an example is how to use sources critically, such as a painting from a given period.

COMMUNICATING MUSICALLY

Teachers need to be confident in taking part in musical activities with children at however simple a level. This involves drawing on wider skills of interacting and communicating with children transferred into a musical context. Singing or playing with the children need not involve performing *for* them, but if teachers can take part in a way which demonstrates their own musical involvement and response, this is a great encouragement to the children to do the same. In itself, this attitude can raise the standard of children's work.

Many adults undervalue their own musical responsiveness. It may help some teachers to reflect on the extent of their past musical involvement, whether as listeners or as practical participants; most people have more experience than they realize. It may also help teachers to think of the approach they take to story reading with children and their readiness in

181

this context to animate the story and communicate with the children through it.

Teachers need to be able to plan and provide for music learning of an ongoing kind for the class and for each child. The skills here are those of seeing how an aspect of music can be 'chunked' or staged into manageable and appropriate pieces for the children concerned and a sequence of work developed. This planning will be done on the basis of the school's planning for music generally and with the support of whatever resources the school has. It is important though for teachers to take control of the detailed planning and provision for music so that it can be tailored to meet children's immediate needs and can make flexible use of time and resources. This needs stressing particularly if a music scheme is in use; any scheme will need adapting and supplementing for use in a particular situation and teachers should feel confident to do this.

Planning for music is no different from planning for other subjects. It cannot be done in the abstract as something apart from a teacher's knowledge and observation of the children. Teachers unused to teaching music understandably find difficulty in planning for it because they lack the experience of children's range of musical capabilities. Once they are carrying out teaching with the children, planning becomes much easier. As a beginning, encouragement to try activities and plan next stages on the basis of observation is the soundest strategy. Support may also be needed for teachers to extend their familiarity with the musical 'map', that is, the range of activities and requirements which make up the basic music curriculum.

ASSESSING PROGRESS AND MATCHING DEVELOPMENTAL NEEDS

Skills of assessing children's progress using these to identify and match developmental needs are directly transferable across the curriculum. The particular application of these within music largely relates back to the skills of listening to children's work. Wider observation skills and the teacher's knowledge of any child as an individual enrich assessment and it is in these respects that a child's own class teacher can often assess and match more effectively than anyone else.

Teachers may initially need help with what kinds of progression to look for and what the indicators might be. This knowledge can be built up by staff together over time. Initially a staff meeting set aside to look at examples of work from across the range of musical activity can be very effective in setting out some general signposts.

Strategies for co-ordinating music

This section looks at a number of strategies which might be used as part of a subject leader's role in developing music in a school. Bearing in mind that every school situation is different, the music co-ordinator will have to decide which ways of carrying out the role are most appropriate to the school, its stage of development and the overall style of management and approach to curriculum responsibilities. The following strategies address key areas within these responsibilities, but they are intended as indicative rather than exhaustive.

AUDITING AND MONITORING

On taking over the role of co-ordinator and at intervals from then on, it will be necessary to find out about the current state of music in the school and how it is developing. The co-ordinator will have a number of impressions, but any action to be taken should be based on more substantial evidence. In addition, the co-ordinator needs to gather the viewpoints of others involved: the headteacher, colleagues, children, assistants, parents. An effective way to collect such evidence is to plan a well-targeted audit and use a range of methods to collect information which can lead to a more realistic picture of the state of affairs.

An audit may target one aspect of the subject, such as composing in Years 5–6, or it may take a wider view, such as asking how music is currently being taught in each class. The following list outlines some areas which it may be useful to investigate as part of an initial audit:

- *People:* What are the musical strengths and interests of colleagues/parents/assistants? What do the children bring musically from home, families, outside activities?
- *Attitudes:* What are teachers' attitudes, feelings and values regarding music?
- *Current teaching and learning:* What does music for each class consist of at the moment? What teaching approaches are being used? What differentiation is there? What progression? What continuity?
- *National Curriculum:* How does the scope of music taught match National Curriculum requirements? Are there any gaps? Are there areas of strength beyond the requirements?
- *Assessment:* What kind of assessment takes place? Are children involved in self-assessment? How is work saved, displayed, discussed? What kind of recording and reporting takes place?

- *Equal opportunities:* Are issues of balance, involvement, curriculum content and children's needs addressed in relation to ability, race, gender and religion?
- *Extra-curricular activity:* What takes place? Who does it cater for? How is learning in this context linked to other music learning?
- *Ethos:* How might the school ethos for music be characterized?
- *Documentation:* What is the current state of documentation for music? Is it effective?

In asking such questions, the co-ordinator needs to identify what kinds of indicators would help to answer them. For example, values regarding music are indicated not only by what people say but also by what they do, how work is presented, when music takes place and so on. Planning an audit includes being clear what is being looked for and how it is to be found. Methods of finding out might include:

- talking to colleagues, management, children, parents, informally or with a questionnaire;
- visiting classrooms, observing, looking at music areas and displays;
- listening to, or looking at, examples of children's work;
- looking at documentation, planning, records.

Clearly each of these methods might be found threatening or intrusive by other teachers and considerable sensitivity and powers of negotiation are required as well as good planning. Finding time to carry out such activity is hard and the whole process needs to be clear, professional and shared with colleagues. The benefits are enormous, however, and even if undertaken in small stages over a long time-scale auditing can pay dividends in leading to effective future action. As curriculum development continues, similar longer-term strategies for monitoring progress or identifying new needs can become built into an ongoing pattern. Waters (1996, p. 15) suggests that:

> Curriculum monitoring is a key element of curriculum leadership. It should be overt, supportive, and developmental. It should extend understanding of the subject area and its teaching.

PLANNING FOR DEVELOPMENT

Any process of auditing and monitoring will raise a number of issues needing thought and discussion. The stage of reflecting on findings is crucial and this often raises further questions. However, after discussion with the headteacher and staff as a whole, it should be possible to group some issues together or to prioritize so that a set of pointers towards future action is identified.

> For example, it may have been discovered that composition takes place only occasionally and is limited to class bouts of quick group pieces, hurriedly listened to but not recorded. This may be linked to several teachers' feeling that the activity isn't worthwhile because the children's work sounds messy. It may also be linked to problems of access to instruments so that when the instruments do appear, children make such a noise that the situation becomes chaotic.

The issues underlying this may be:

- the need for quiet places for music hasn't been addressed;
- there is no ongoing provision for access to instruments one or two at a time for skill practice;
- lack of skills in using instruments causes difficulties in composition;
- groups for composition are so large that the children either compromise their ideas or give up;
- teachers are unclear what they're listening for;
- because no work is saved or talked through, children assume it doesn't matter much and don't take it seriously.

This is a long list and action will need to be planned on a long-term basis. Decisions need to be made about what order to tackle things in and a plan made with short-, medium- and long-term goals identified. In the above example, tackling any one of the issues would probably begin to unlock the rest but this is not always so. Judging what to tackle first may be related to other issues, of resources, demands on time or school priorities as a whole.

At this stage it also becomes necessary to consider what kinds of activity will be effective in supporting development towards the desired goals. Available strategies might be:

- time in a staff meeting for discussion or input from the co-ordinator or others; time in a staff meeting for a short practical activity with teaching/learning points highlighted;
- more substantial INSET led by the co-ordinator or a visitor;
- collaborative teaching or planning or both, with or without the co-ordinator;
- time for the co-ordinator to visit other schools, attend courses, organize resources.

WORKING WITH COLLEAGUES

One of the most interesting and potentially effective ways of developing practice is through collaborative work with colleagues. At best this benefits both teachers as the opportunity to exchange ideas or to work side by side nearly always leads to new possibilities emerging for both. If its potential is to be seen through into real change, however, such work must be planned for and set up on a thoroughly professional basis. A mistake often made is to make such collaborations as informal as possible on grounds that this will keep it all non-threatening. In fact, this doesn't follow, and such ventures often founder for lack of time, clear aims, or even the inappropriate feeling the co-ordinator may end up with that colleagues are 'doing me a favour' by trying a new way of working.

Collaborative work with colleagues demands both professional and interpersonal skills of the co-ordinator. In music, for all the reasons explored earlier in the book, there may be added dimensions of personal discomfort with the subject as well as professional lack of knowledge. The most sound basis for setting up a collaboration is a situation in which a colleague asks for such support, perhaps as a result of an auditing process which has identified problems. Above all, the work should be planned with the support of senior management. It should be recognized as a form of INSET and time must be found for meetings and/or joint work with children. Without such recognition the chances of success are considerably lessened.

As part of the planning stages, the co-ordinator and colleague will need to meet to agree an overall aim for the work and three sets of short-term goals:

- for the children;
- for the teacher;
- for the co-ordinator.

The overall aim will relate to the school's plans for developing music and to the particular teacher's role. Continuing the example above, for instance, it might be agreed that a Year 3 teacher will work on composition with his own class with the co-ordinator's support. The overall aim is to establish a good start in composition for children entering Key Stage 2, which the teacher will later share with the Year 4 teacher to whom the children will transfer at the end of the year. Goals for the children are that at least half the class will have worked on an individual or paired composition of their own, finished and saved it on tape, and appraised it with the class by the end of the term. Goals for the teacher are to implement the organization of this and to develop the skills of listening to the children's work. Goals for the co-ordinator are that a model is set up which can be adapted by other teachers who will be encouraged by the children's success and enjoyment.

Once aims and goals are clear, the practical plans for work can be made. Collaboration may be carried out by meeting to plan, teaching separately or together, or one teaching and one observing (either way round). Whatever the format, time to talk is indispensable. Opportunity to discuss issues arising and to review work against goals is essential; finding this time can be the greatest challenge of all. Just as in the classroom children are encouraged to be aware of their own learning, so in working with adults it is important for both to be aware of the process of development itself and to have the opportunity to identify and evaluate learning. The co-ordinator will also need to evaluate his/her own role in the process and may face a number of issues arising. The following list indicates some areas for consideration by the co-ordinator as work develops:

- How far are musical aims and goals being met? In what ways? Have other considerations come to light which have required plans to be adapted?
- What are the differences in teaching style between you? These may show in interaction with pupils, classroom organization, attitude, pace and so on. Were you able to adapt your ideas and musical approaches to fit into your colleague's teaching style? Were you able to find common ground?
- How successfully were you able to involve your colleague in all decision-making? Were you able to plan and work to your colleague's musical strengths and capabilities?
- What insights have you gained into adult learning needs and learning styles (your own and your colleague's)?
- What scope has there been for real change in relation to music teaching and learning? Whose change? What will be the indicators of this in the children's learning long-term? What will your long-term role be in facilitating and monitoring this?
- Were there any issues of conflict? Was it possible to resolve these or use conflict constructively?
- Were there any issues of control, power or status? Where were the inequalities between you, e.g. in experience, age, level of responsibility? Did these matter?
- Were there any issues of communication? To what extent were you understanding each other?
- What did you observe of your colleague's competence? How well did this tie up with your colleague's self-assessment?

- How did your role emerge? What did you *actually* do? How would you evaluate your work? How would your colleague evaluate your work?
- What conclusions would you draw about collaborative work as part of (a) professional development and (b) music curriculum development?

Given the widespread lack of time in initial training for music, collaborative work between the co-ordinator and other teachers can go a long way towards establishing a basis for developing work with children, particularly if the work includes teaching together. It is essential for teachers to see and hear music in action in order to gain a sense of the children's responses as well as the practicalities of how to manage the situation. Music is transient in itself, invisible, and hard to catch hold of in order to discuss it. Shared experiences of music with children can help by giving a common basis on which to discuss aspects of their learning.

WHOLE STAFF INSET

Whilst some needs identified by an auditing process may be individual, others can more effectively be addressed by the staff as a group together. The co-ordinator may need to plan and lead INSET for colleagues as part of the music curriculum development programme for the school. The role here requires a fine balance between a willingness on the one hand to take a lead, give information, show and lead practical activities, and introduce ideas, vocabulary and teaching strategies where necessary, and on the other hand to discover and use each staff member's own skills and resources, co-ordinate discussion which draws on everybody's contributions, and facilitate other people's innovative ideas and initiatives. It is worth remembering just how crucial *musically* the latter aspect is. As individuals everyone has their own musical responsiveness and it is this which energizes teaching interactions with children. This has to be seen within the context of creative work generally and the more teachers are in touch with their own musical sense and feel comfortable drawing on it, the more they can help children to do the same.

In relation to the teaching skills identified earlier in this chapter, it is often listening skills which are overlooked. Teachers understandably want to know what to *do* with the children. A much more key concern if work is to progress is that teachers know *how to listen* and *what to listen for*. It can be useful to bear this in mind when planning staff INSET. The emphasis in any practical activity or in discussing examples of children's work needs to be on what to listen for, how to listen, listening as an aspect of observation and so on. Developing teachers' listening skills and confidence can have a wide-ranging effect on the quality of music teaching.

A strategy which can be useful if a number of staff identify themselves as beginners in music teaching is to plan a teaching focus to be carried out in every class at the same time. For example, for a four-week period every class in the school might work on the idea of music based in some way on repeated rhythm patterns. Work is planned as a whole staff, with each teacher contributing, selecting or adapting teaching ideas from a central 'pool' into which the co-ordinator can feed ideas and resources. Teachers might work quite separately or together at times; visiting artists (for example, a drumming group or a composer) might lead workshop sessions; a common vocabulary is collected and established, listening examples are gathered and swapped. As work progresses, children in one class might visit one another as audiences or performers, perhaps just for ten minutes before lunch. The strength of this as INSET is that it not only generates ideas and group support but that it also enables teachers to begin to evolve a developmental picture as they see the way work unfolds with each age-group and with children who are more or less experienced.

In any subject area, there is value in staff development experiences taking place as a whole group. In music there is one step further where this might be taken. If staff have opportunities to make music together in however light-hearted a way, this adds a whole extra dimension of quality to the sense of music in the school which forms the background to children's work. The idea may terrify some and seem an unaffordable luxury to others, but it may be worth keeping in the back of the co-ordinator's mind.

WRITING SCHEMES OF WORK

There is no point in a co-ordinator preparing a scheme of work for music until there is a reasonably consistent school-wide practice of teaching it. Drawing up a scheme of work is often seen as a strategy belonging to the early stages of curriculum development. It can turn into a meaningless and redundant paper exercise if it is devised by the co-ordinator alone and represents hopes rather than realities.

To be useful a scheme of work needs to be *descriptive* as well as *prescriptive*. It doesn't invent or imagine what might or could happen. It outlines what does and can happen. This has implications for how the scheme of work is evolved in relation to staff and curriculum development in music. Nor can the scheme 'fix' problems the school has in music; it only makes sense in relation to some agreed and understood

189

practice with which staff are familiar and confident. So writing the scheme of work should involve plenty of consultation and should be planned for but not carried out until the school is ready. Pateman (1996) recommends forming a music planning group, representative of all years and a range of teaching skills. Thought also needs to be given to what *can* be outlined in a scheme of work and what cannot; also to what can *usefully* be outlined? A scheme can clarify the main aims and intended learning outcomes for children's learning in music. It can outline the teaching content, approaches and resources which are to be used in reaching these; and it can suggest units, groupings and sequences of work for those aspects of the subject where this makes sense, for example, by indicating a focus on music of a particular genre, time or place. It can hold together a joint vision based on thoughtful provision, and give overall guidance as to the ground that is to be covered year by year.

A scheme of work cannot, however, stand in for initial training teachers never had. It cannot give lesson plans and resources for all work to be carried out. Above all, it cannot ensure that progression in learning takes place since this depends on the teacher who observes and responds to pupils, matching task to need. Quality learning depends on a good match between pupils' needs (skills, knowledge, understanding) and opportunities offered. The scheme will need to indicate assessment points and give some guidance of what to look for in relation to any unit of work carried out. It should also assume that teachers will adapt plans and allow room for this to happen.

There are some aspects of music, as there are of language, where work follows an ongoing individual pathway. Learning an instrument, either in individual lessons or through an extra-curricular group, and building up individual experience of composing both need to be treated in a way that is somewhat akin to planning for and monitoring writing development. The scheme of work should take account of this and clarify how these key aspects of music are to be managed and tracked for each child and how they can be flexibly related to class-work.

MANAGING RESOURCES

The co-ordinator has the remit to manage and often to purchase music resources for the school. This is a key part of the role, though it may seem fairly mundane. Resource collections carry messages; they influence pedagogy; and they can help or hinder the development of music in the school. The following checklist might be applied in evaluating resources of all kinds: collections of recordings, books, songbooks, instruments and schemes.

Resources evaluation checklist:

Curriculum relevance:

1 Check and define scope against National Curriculum expectations.
2 Check and define scope against school's aims, policy and scheme of work.

Implicit pedagogy:

3 What teaching/learning strategies and approaches are implicit or explicit? Are these 'congruent' with the ways you would want to work? If not, can the differences be managed?

Curriculum progression and continuity:

4 For which age-group does use of this resource fit best? What is its level of 'difficulty'? How well does it mesh with existing frameworks for progression and continuity? How well does it allow for differentiation between individual children? for special needs of any kind?

Staff use:

5 How does the resource meet staff needs?
6 How much preparation time does its use demand?

(Differentiate between individual colleagues in addressing these questions.)

Equal opportunities:

7 What breadth of ethnic and cultural coverage does it offer, or where does this resource fit into your overall coverage?
8 What gender, racial or religious bias or stereotypes does the resource have?

PUBLISHED MUSIC SCHEMES

Following the advent of the National Curriculum for music there has been a proliferation of commercially produced music schemes for Key Stages 1 and 2 by almost all the major educational publishers. These are often very substantial collections designed to provide a whole package of lessons with teachers' guidance and resources, including books, tapes, compact discs, copiable worksheets, pictures and charts. Such materials are admirable in their way and obviously are proving to be successful in giving a prop to those who are uncertain. They frequently provide some good materials in the form of songs and music for listening. However, the co-ordinator needs to be aware of some of the dangers of investing large amounts of the music budget and investing a total commitment to such materials.

191

First, used in their entirety as a sequenced progression of musical activities they can replace the teacher's planning for the specific needs of the children in the class. Like commercial mathematics schemes, music schemes predetermine the content of children's musical experiences in a way which does not allow for the children's initiation or the development or musical activities which are governed by the child's particular interests or requirements. There is also the danger of the scheme underestimating children's abilities in order to increase safety for the teacher. Ideally, the teacher should select materials which are appropriate to the children's stage of development.

Second, the materials can be seen to *replace* the teacher: CDs provide the singing and teaching points. As in the use of old radio broadcasts for music, this can limit the children's responses and prevents the flexibility of approach which is needed in teaching anything.

Third, and perhaps most importantly, such materials often convey a double message which may, unwittingly, diminish teachers' confidence: the first message is that 'non-specialists will be able to do music if they use this scheme'; the second message is that 'non-specialists cannot do music without such a scheme'. This negates what we have argued throughout this book: that teachers are able, using their own musical knowledge and experience coupled with their general teaching skills, to teach the primary music curriculum. While any good musical materials are valuable, we should not lose sight of the aim set out by the Music National Curriculum Working Party that music, like all other subjects, should be under the firm control of the class teacher.

References

Alexander, R., Rose, J. and Woodhead, C. (1992) *Curriculum Organisation and Classroom Practice in Primary Schools: A Discussion Paper*. London: DES.

Campbell, R. (1985) *Developing the Primary Curriculum*. London: Holt, Rinehart and Winston.

DES and Welsh Office (1991) *National Curriculum Music Working Group: Interim Report*. London: DES.

Galton, M. (1996) Teaching, learning and the co-ordinator. In J. O'Neill and N. Kitson (eds), *Effective Curriculum Management*. London: Routledge.

Mills, J. (1994) Music in the National Curriculum: The First Year. *British Journal of Music Education* 11 (30), 191–6.

OFSTED (1995) *Music: A Review of Inspection Findings*. London: HMSO.

Pateman, M. (1996) Planning a scheme of work for music. *Primary Music Today*, issues 6, 7.

Plummeridge, C. (1991) *Music Education in Theory and Practice*.

Rowland, S. (1984) *The Enquiring Classroom*. London: Falmer.

Waters, M. (1996) *Curriculum Co-ordinators in Primary Schools.* London: Collins Educational.

Wragg, E.C., Bennett, S.N. and Carré, C.G. (1989) *Primary teachers and the National Curriculum.* Research Papers in Education, nos 3, 4, 17, 37.

Musical Instruments for the Primary Classroom
Compiled by Susan Young

Instruments for striking

Tuned percussion:	xylophones	all notes
	glockenspiels	all notes
	chime bars	all notes
	metallophones	all notes
	gato drum (tongue drum)	

Untuned percussion:	wood blocks
	claves
	gong-gong
	cymbals (one large, preferably on stand)
	gongs
	bells (various sizes)
	triangles (one large)
	drums: bongos, tambours, tabla drums, snare drums
	(many sizes and shapes)
Strikers:	beaters of various materials: felt, rubber, wood, plastic metal strikers, thick and thin (for metal instruments)
	brushes

Instruments for scraping

Guiro:	temple bowls, wine glasses
Bowed instruments:	violin, viola, cellos, double bass

Many instruments produce sounds by scraping carefully with beaters or hands.

Instruments for shaking
Maracas (preferably wooden, or gourds)
Cabasa
Tubo
Seed pods (many shapes and sizes)

Anklets and bracelets (of bells or seeds)
Tambourines

Instruments for blowing
Recorders (whole family)
Ocarina
Mouth organ
Small pipes and whistles of many sizes and materials

Instruments for plucking
Zithers
Harps and autoharps
Guitars
Inside of the piano
Sitar
Sansa, mbira

Electronic instruments
MIDI (Musical Instrument Digital Interface) keyboards with drum-pad assigning and multi-track sequencing facility

Drum machine

Computer and software for composing, sequencing – if possible, MIDI-linked to keyboard from which it can sample sounds of quality

Piano
One of the most exciting pieces of musical equipment in schools is the piano. All schools have one, if not more than one; yet they often remain closed to children. There is no reason why the piano should not be a part of the children's battery of instruments for exploration.

Modified Instruments
for children with physical disabilities.

Further Resources

The following list gives an indication of some of the available smaller-scale resources which may be useful in supplementing the approaches to music described in this book.

Bagenal, A. and M. (1993) *Music from the Past.* (Four books linked to National Curriculum history Topics.)

Bright Ideas Teachers Handbooks (1987) *Language Resources.* Leamington Spa: Scholastic.

Catherall, E. (1989) *Exploring Sound.* Hove: Wayland.

Connolly, Y., Cameron, G. and Singham, S. (1981) *Mango Spice: 44 Caribbean Songs.* London: A. & C. Black.

Cotton, M. (1996) *Agogo Bells to Xylophone: A Friendly Guide to Classroom Percussion Instruments.* A. & C. Black.

Davies, L. (1985) *Sound Waves.* London: Bell & Hyman.

Davies, L. (1994) *Take Note.*

East, H. (1989) *The Singing Sack: Songs from Around the World.* London: A. & C. Black.

East, H. (1990) *Look Lively, Rest Easy: Stories, Songs, Tricks and Rhymes.* London: A. & C. Black.

Floyd, L. (1980) *Indian Music.* London: OUP.

Gilbert, J. (1981) *Musical Starting Points with Young Children.* London: Ward Lock Educational.

Holdstock, J. (1986) *Earwiggo up, Earwiggo down: Pitch games.* Produced by Yorkshire and Humberside Association for Music in Special Education. Distributed by Ray Lovely Music, Tadcaster.

Magee, W. (1989) *Madtail, Miniwhale and Other Shape Poems.* London: Viking/ Kestrel.

Mantra's Multicultural Book of Songs. London: Mantra.

McGregor, H. (1995) *Listening to Music.* London: A. & C. Black.

Microsoft (CD-Rom) *Musical Instruments.*

Pettigrew, M. (1990) *Simply Science: Music and Sound.* London: Franklin Watts.

Pugh, A. (1991) *Women in Music.* Cambridge: CUP.

Richards, C. (1990) *Ways into Music.* (Four books of musical activities.)

Shepherd, M. (1989) *Music is Childsplay: Shared Learning Activities.* Harlow: Longman.

Shreeves, R. (1990) *Children Dancing* (2nd edition). East Grinstead: Ward Lock Educational.

Ward, H. (1996) *Franzo Frog and Friends: A Beginner's Course for Descant Recorder.* Oxford: Heinemann.

Index

Index